YOU
CAN MAKE A
DIFFERENCE!

Helping Others and
Yourself Through Volunteering

MARLENE WILSON

Published by
Volunteer Management Associates
320 South Cedar Brook Road
Boulder, Colorado 80304

Other Books by the Author

The Effective Management of Volunteer Programs

Survival Skills for Managers

How to Mobilize Church Volunteers

Edited and designed by Lisa K. Wilson

Cover design by Molly Gough

Copyright © 1990 by Marlene Wilson

Library of Congress Catalog Card Number: 90-70355

ISBN: 0-9603362-3-0

To Harvey—

With love and gratitude

Contents

7: Sharing Your Lifetime Experience / 115

A healthy attitude is the key—Volunteering is good for your health—Sharing expertise and experience—How retirees are helping—Volunteering as a group activity—How to get started volunteering

8: Giving to Others When You Have Less / 131

The myth of helpers and helpees—Giving: When you're disabled—Giving: When you're chronically ill

9: Impacting the Future / 143

Understanding the past—The present: Who's volunteering?—Looking toward the future—A call to action

Acknowledgments

I am glad that tradition provides this forum for publicly thanking those special people who helped this book become a reality. For me, writing is a paradox—a mixture of loving it and hating it; of intense solitude and grateful community; and of personal beliefs freely expressed and needing the objective and loving scrutiny of trusted others.

So it is to those trusted others, who invested so much time and careful attention to reviewing my manuscript, that I am deeply grateful. Betty Stallings, Doris Pierson, Jane Justis, Sheila Albert, Charles Zablocki, Ruth Hattendorf, Vicki Hamer, and Arlene Schindler—these colleagues offered me wise counsel, shared stories, and objectively critiqued the format and content. Thank you all.

I am also deeply grateful to VOLUNTEER: The National Center for so graciously sharing the information about the President's Volunteer Action Award winners and citationists. These stories of quiet heroes across our country greatly enriched the book.

But most of all, I am deeply grateful to my editor, Lisa Wilson. I have always loved and valued Lisa deeply as my daughter, but working together on this project gave me an opportunity to develop a deep respect and appreciation for her as a consummate professional. She is the finest editor I have ever worked with—intuitively knowing when to push, support, change, or accept, always with the goal of creating the finest book possible. She has been a joy to work with in this partnership.

And finally, thanks to my son Richard for his cheering from the sidelines, and the much-needed reminders to smell the roses along the way.

Preface

There is good news in America! That is important information for those whose steady diet of newspapers and telecasts have begun to make them believe that the vast majority of Americans are either involved in crime, drugs, dishonesty, or violent behavior or at best are indifferent to them.

It is true our society has all of these problems, and unfortunately in many communities they are escalating. What is not true is that most of our citizens are either involved in creating these problems or uninvolved in searching for solutions.

In my opinion, it is time that the "good news" stories are heard. There are, in fact, more people giving significantly of their time, energy, and resources to improve the quality of life in this country than ever before—and many of them are doing it as volunteers, which means they are not being paid for their efforts. These quiet heroes are in every town and city and they are 80 million strong. They contributed 19.5 billion hours of voluntary effort worth $150 billion in 1987 alone (according to the 1987 Gallup Survey "Giving and Volunteering in the United States"). These numbers indicate over 45 percent of adult Americans not only *do* care, but have invested their time and energy to prove it. That is not just good news, it's incredible news!

Why do people work hard for causes they care about without even getting paid for doing it? That question is often asked of volunteers, and there is no simple answer. Each volunteer has his or her own unique reason for being involved.

Deciding to volunteer is a very personal commitment and covers the vast range of causes, concerns, beliefs, attitudes, and needs of our richly diverse populace. It may not be for everyone, but when close to half our adult population is involved in it, it's worth carefully examining the "why." Volunteering just might be what you have been searching for—to help you find more meaning and purpose for your life.

This book is a celebration of today's volunteers, and a primer for prospective volunteers. Why people volunteer, and how; what they receive as well as what they give; when it makes sense for you to seriously consider helping others as a volunteer, and how to go about it . . . these are all explored in these pages.

The one common theme almost universally agreed upon by volunteers of all ages and types is this: the one who gets the most out of it is the volunteer! You get back far more than you can ever give. This is the wonderful paradox of volunteering.

Each chapter addresses a different life situation in which volunteering may be a viable option for you or someone you care about. There are wonderful, real-life examples throughout the book of what ordinary people like you and your own family, friends, and neighbors are doing for others—and how they are making a significant difference. You can too!

I want to add a personal note about the writing of this book. It was when I was in the midst of preparing this manuscript that my husband Harvey was struck and killed by a truck. In an instant my whole life changed and I struggled with the notion of dropping or postponing the book indefinitely. But I knew this project was one Harvey was very excited about, believing, as I do, that it's message is needed *now*. So, I decided to continue and dedicate the book to Harvey—my husband, partner, best cheerleader, and most honest critic for 33 wonderful years.

It is one of the most beautiful compensations of this life that no man can sincerely try to help another without helping himself.

—Ralph Waldo Emerson

—•1•—

Bringing More Joy and Fulfillment to Your Life

To love what you do and feel that it matters—how could anything be more fun?

—*Kathryn Graham*

Has it ever occurred to you, as it has to me, that *more* does not necessarily mean *better*? More money, more things, more activities, more time—none of these guarantees more happiness, fulfillment, or meaning in life. Phillip Berman, in his book *The Courage of Conviction*, summarizes this idea well: "It seems important to bear in mind that it is entirely possible to be wealthy with things and yet, at the same time, intellectually and spiritually impoverished."

It is also an interesting paradox that *less* does not equate with *better* either. Less responsibility, less money, less activity—these are not necessarily the ways to find more joy in life.

I'd like to help you explore some *different* ways of using whatever you have in the way of time, abilities, and resources to bring new fulfillment and joy to your life.

What Does it Mean to be Joyful?

At first glance, this may seem to be an absurd question. Yet, I have found that many people today don't use the word joy anymore—they either feel it is too religious or outmoded. I think that's sad, and I've wondered why that is. The following story by the renowned author, philosopher, and theologian Henri Nouwen, helps explain this concern:

> I vividly remember how one of my university teachers spoke a whole year about anxiety in human life. He discussed in great detail the thoughts of Kierkegaard, Sarte, Heidegger, and Camus and gave an impressive exposé of the anatomy of fear. One day, during the last month of the course, a few students found the courage to interrupt him and ask him to speak a little about joy before the course was over. At first he was taken aback, but then he promised to give it a try. The next class he started hesitantly to speak about joy. His words sounded less convincing and penetrating than when he spoke about anxiety and fear. Finally, after two more meetings, he told us that he had run out of ideas about joy and would continue his interrupted train of thought. This event made a deep impression on me, especially since I had such great admiration for my teacher. I kept asking myself why he was unable to teach about joy as eloquently as he had taught about anxiety.[1]

Unfortunately, this is not only true in the classroom, but also in the media. We are bombarded day in and day out with negative news. And since we now have the marvel of satellites and mass communications, we can share bad news from all over the world. As one reader said in a letter to the editor of *The Washington Post* (May 20, 1989):

> During World War II, my favorite news program was Gabriel Heatter, whose lead in was *"there's good news tonight."* Today I'm hard put to find much good news in

the media. You seem concerned primarily with scandals, swindles, theft at high levels, rape, child abuse, dope, and murder.

The comics are un-funny . . . The sports pages (which used to be pleasant reading) now highlight infractions, gambling, cocaine, strikes and feet of clay. The business section warns of coming recession, the threat of high interest rates, and the Japanese invasion. *Wouldn't it be original and refreshing to print a Good News section—if you could find anything to fill it?* (Italics mine.)

The reality is, there *are* inspiring, incredible "good news" stories in every community happening every single day. Part of the purpose of this book is to share some of those stories and to show how many people find not only fulfillment, but joy through volunteering.

When I was working on the revision of this chapter I tried to find another word for joy which would convey what I wanted to say—I couldn't find one. There is no other word quite like it. Joy is a good word that needs to regain its place in our modern vocabulary. It means delight, happiness, jubilance, elation, exhilaration. That is exactly what I believe volunteering can bring into your life.

Our best teachers in this business of living joyfully are those who simply do it! We all know people who radiate a serene acceptance of their situation, whether they are rich or poor, young or old, well or sick. They accept their lives, but not in a stoic or passive way. They live their lives to the fullest, and experience great joy in the process, no matter what their circumstance might be. It feels good just to be around them.

The one characteristic these remarkable people seem to share is a genuine concern for others, not just for themselves—in being givers and not just takers in life. This is the essence of volunteering.

I had the pleasure of meeting such a person at the Arkansas State Conference on Volunteerism in 1989. Her name is Jo Ann Cayce, and she had been presented a President's Volunteer Action Citation in 1989. (Note: The President's Volunteer Action Awards and Citations were created in 1982. To date, there have been 139 recipients of this prestigious award. This program is cosponsored by VOLUNTEER: The National Center and ACTION in cooperation with the White House Office of National Service. In 1989 alone there were 2,000 nominations received.)

I sat next to "Miz Cayce," as she is affectionately called, at the awards luncheon and have never met a person more enthusiastic about what she's doing. She literally bubbled over with stories of the rural Arkansas people she's spent more than 30 years working with as a volunteer. "It just came naturally," she said. "My grandma did it and my mama after her—so of course, I learned how to share from them. I love these people!"

The state health and welfare officials at the conference later told me Jo Ann personally provides her own kind of "safety net" for people in seven counties who fall through the cracks of the system. This means she provides needed clothing, food, transportation to medical appointments, and just about anything else these people need. Her husband was also at the awards luncheon, and I asked him what he thought about his wife's volunteer work: "More than once I've seen a pair of shoes I couldn't find or a suit I thought I had walk down the street on someone else," he chuckled. "But I figure, if she gave it to them, they needed it more than I did!" The Cayce's are a wonderful example of ordinary people making an extraordinary difference and experiencing great joy in the process.

There are many people like Jo Ann Cayce who have been raised in families with deeply-held values about giving and volunteering. Reaching out to others is natural for them. They don't regard it as anything special. Their motto seems to be "If someone's in need and you can help, you just do it."

What a treasure these people are to any family or community. My hope is that they keep passing on that generous spirit to their children, and to their children's children, because it has never been more needed than in today's hurting world.

A friend of mine, Betty Stallings, has not only been involved in volunteering all her life, but has also found volunteering with her husband and two daughters to be both meaningful and great fun.

> When we were a young family, we frequently became involved in activities in which several of us could be involved. For example, we worked as a family at Special Olympics on days when they were doing sports our children were involved in. I still remember our daughter's deep, emotional response after attending her first Special Olympics awards ceremony. She said she didn't know whether to laugh or cry at the ceremony. We also visited a man in a convalescent hospital who had no family or visitors. It was a great family activity to visit our adopted grandpa, and we even included our dog. We were also the American foreign host family for four different families who lived in Berkeley while a member of their family attended the University of California at Berkeley. It was a great way to add cultural diversity to our children's lives, and the relationships are still very special. We have continued to have reunions with them in their countries and ours. I think that volunteering as a family helps to cultivate young people as the volunteers of the future.

These are activities any family can do that not only help others, but also build stronger, healthier, more joyful relationships between parents and children. It is also a wonderful option for single parents who are looking for ways to enrich their relationship with their children on weekend or holiday visits.

Giving—a Way to Feel Useful

The need to be needed and to feel useful is a powerful human motivation. In fact, according to the survey conducted by the Gallup Organization, "Giving and Volunteering in the United States," more than one-half (56 percent) of the 80 million people who volunteered in 1987, gave *wanting to do something useful* as their primary reason for volunteering. The other reasons most commonly given were:[2]

- **Thought they would enjoy the work**
- **A family member or friend would benefit**
- **For religious reasons**

In other, less complex and sophisticated times, this need to be useful was almost automatically met. Children helped out on the farm or in the family business. Grandparents provided support and caring for the youngsters because they often lived in the same house or nearby. Workers pitched in and did whatever needed to be done without the restraints of formal job descriptions or union agreements. And small town and rural residents saw to it that their neighbors' needs were met. It was called "pitching in," "helping out," or "lending a hand,"and it was a beautiful and spontaneous form of volunteering.

There are, of course, people who still find ways to do this kind of volunteering wherever they are. And there are places where this kind of helping still takes place, but it is most apt to occur in rural communities, small towns, and ethnic neighborhoods. I once read a heartwarming story in *The Denver Post* about ranchers in the Gunnison River Valley in Colorado and how they helped each other:

"Neighborliness is as much a part of the lifestyle in ranch country as blue jeans . . . It can be as simple as giving an unexpected plate of cinnamon rolls, or as tough as calving for a sick neighbor. Sometimes it's asked for, usually not."

The article described one woman who was called away because her father was hurt in an accident. She had just begun painting the living room when she got the call. When she returned four days later, the house was painted and cleaned by her neighbors. And when one rancher went off to help fight the Yellowstone National Park forest fires in 1988, friends cut and baled his hay.

No one keeps score of such acts. There is no balance sheet. "What goes around comes around," one rancher said.[3]

I grew up in a small Montana town of less than 1,000 people, so reading that article brought back a flood of memories for me. For example, my mother was a wonderful cook and at Christmas time would delight in baking an array of Scandinavian goodies. My brother, Ralph, and I always knew that on Christmas Eve we would spend a couple of hours pulling our sleds all over town delivering those wonderful, homemade delights to every widow, widower, and shut-in. It was always one of the most joyful parts of the holidays.

In small communities word gets around when someone is in need. But in most urban and suburban communities, life is not that simple. (According to the 1989 census, *more than 75 percent* of the people in the U.S. now live in cities or suburban areas, and nearly half the U.S. population lives in the 37 biggest metro areas.) People in these areas still need to feel needed and useful, but finding out who needs help has become more difficult. Additionally, we are a very mobile society, and one of the unfortunate results is that we are too often a society of strangers. This national change of lifestyle and the shift from rural to urban living has impacted all aspects of our lives, including volunteering.

The kind of giving that brings joy and fulfillment in today's world is beautifully depicted by these two personal stories from the book *Ordinary People as Monks and Mystics*, by Marsha Sinetar:

A retired woman had been an accountant for many years, and was also deeply involved in community and church volunteering. She said:

> Now that I'm retired, I can give all my time to service and church-related projects . . . I don't give of myself because I "should"—I don't like the word "should" because that makes me feel I have to do something, and takes the joy out of it for me. I'm just selfishly doing what makes me happy.

And a young male environmentalist talked about his work for causes he cared about:

> If I were to describe the personal attributes that have helped me be happy and productive, I'd say my caring for others lets me be happy. This feeling is grounded in an optimism and what I call a gentleness for all life. Caring for others and the environment fills me with happiness.[4]

How Volunteers are Helping

There is an incredible variety of options open to volunteers today. This makes it possible for people to find something to do that meets a real need and at the same time fits what they like to do or want to learn. This "right match" is what most often brings real fulfillment and joy to the volunteer. The following is just a partial list of volunteer opportunities available to anyone:

VOLUNTEER OPTIONS

Literacy volunteer	Tutor
Hospital volunteer	Crisis phone counselor
School aide	Little League coach
Red Cross disaster volunteer	Blood donor

Child/wife abuse volunteer
Office assistant
Nursing home friend
Recreation instructor
Lap to sit on
School crossing guard
Photographer
Trainer
Meals on Wheels driver
School health aide
Emergency driver
Committee chair or member
Receptionist
Board of directors member
Computer operator
Newsletter editor or writer
Public relations volunteer
Youth leader
Reader for the blind
Humane Society volunteer
Telephone aide
Repair person
Translator
Wheelchair pusher
Foster grandparent
Recycling volunteer
Docent in museum or gallery
Advocate
Gleaner
AIDS care giver
Job readiness trainer
National Parks volunteer
Housing advocate
Rehabilitation volunteer
Suicide hot line counselor
Drug and alcohol counselor
Volunteer fire fighter

Library aide
Speakers bureau member
Crafts or arts teacher
Day care aide
Library aide to shut-in
Zoo volunteer
Graphic artist
Companion to retarded
   or mentally ill
Emergency shelter
   volunteer
Cook or server for
   feeding programs
Computer programmer
Receptionist
Typist
Hospice volunteer
Braille transcriber
Task force leader or
   member
Envelope stuffer
Snow shoveler
Musician
Management consultant
Fund raiser
Nature guide
Theatre group member
Park maintenance and
   planting
Peer counselor
Storyteller
Medical volunteer
IRS tax assistant
Clown
Builder of playground
   equipment
Naturalist

Ham radio operator
Historic buildings renovator
TV and video producer
Gardener
Geologist
Camp counselor
Search and rescue volunteer
Support group leader
Children's court advocate
Victim's assistance aide
Wildlife refuge volunteer
Accountant
Family counselor
Gift shop volunteer
First aid/CPR instructor
Researcher
Evaluator
Home nursing aide
Friendly visitor

Friendly shopper
Public Broadcasting aide
Host for foreign visitors
Neighborhood safety
    programs
Technical assistant
Therapeutic horseback
    riding instructor
Neighborhood mediator
Music, arts, and museum
    guides
Therapeutic swimming
    instructor
Clothing and food bank
    volunteer
Teacher of English as a
    second language
Blood pressure and
    cholesterol screener

And the list could go on . . . and on . . . and on. (See chapter 5 for a listing of volunteer opportunities in religious organizations.)

Where Should You Begin?

How does a person sort through all of these options? Where and how can you begin? *The San Francisco Chronicle* printed an article about the amazing deluge of volunteers in the Bay area (even for difficult causes such as the homeless and AIDS). Included in it was this excellent advice:[5]

TIPS FOR FINDING A VOLUNTEER JOB

1. Narrow the field. Do you like the arts or are you more interested in helping those with AIDS? It's easier to find something rewarding if you know what you're after.

2. Do some research. Find out what's available. Ask friends, check the want ads or call the Volunteer Center in your area.

3. Evaluate your skills. What can you offer that someone might need? Can you program a computer? Can you work during the day? These are both hot assets.

4. Treat it like a job interview. Take a resume if you have one and be prepared to answer questions about your background.

5. Dress appropriately. If you're meeting with the board of directors, wear a suit. If you're going to be serving food in a homeless shelter, more casual clothes are OK.

6. Be flexible. One woman came into the Bay Area Women's Resource Center expecting to attend business forums and solicit clothing donations. She wound up marketing a popular photo exhibit.

7. Choose a regular block of time to volunteer. Offer to work every Wednesday afternoon, for example. This makes it easier for volunteer coordinators to schedule you.

8. Be consistent. Reliable volunteers are in demand and always appreciated.

9. Be patient. Remember, this is not IBM you're dealing with, but a nonprofit organization.

10. If it doesn't work out, try someplace else. There will always be places that need help, and eventually you'll find one where you fit in.

One other suggestion I would add is to watch your newspapers for weekly columns of volunteer opportunities and for human interest stories about voluntary organizations and causes. Also, see Appendix A for a list of Volunteer Centers in the U.S. and Canada.

There are also a growing number of television campaigns highlighting outstanding volunteers and encouraging others to become more involved. Major articles in both local and national newspapers and major magazines are also featuring the subject of volunteering and citizen involvement. The media seems to be discovering the newsworthiness of these stories and, to their credit, are reporting more and more of them. In the process, the whole nation is realizing the mental health benefits of hearing good news. I wholeheartedly applaud these exciting efforts!

Volunteering Can be Just Plain Fun!

One of the delightful things about volunteering today is the enormous variety of opportunities available. Many volunteers are doing what they enjoy most and are having great fun in the process. Here are just a few examples:

—**Elizabeth Cooper Terwilliger** has always had a keen interest in nature and ecology. For more than 30 years she's shared her knowledge and love of the outdoors with Marin County, California, school children. She conducts what she calls "bird-in-the-hand" programs out of a specially equipped van and takes youngsters on hiking, biking, and canoeing nature field trips. She's written several nature books and appeared in a number of nature movies. Now the program has 100 volunteers, 4 salaried naturalists, 3 vans, and impacts 75,000 school children every year, *and* she does what she loves best.

—**Several residents of Bedford, Virginia**, (population 25,000) worked for more than a decade to bring cultural events to their city. They renovated a theatre and formed the *Little Town Players*, a group that involves all ages in producing, staging, and acting in several theatre productions each year. They provide apprentice programs and scholarships for students, have children's theatre and puppet shows for kids, and offer dramatic readings and musical programs for their town's senior citizens. They have built a truly enriching and enjoyable program which touches the lives of hundreds, and they're doing what they most enjoy.

—**The citizens of Gilroy, California,** annually sponsor the Gilroy Garlic Festival, which now involves more than 3,500 volunteers, attracts about 135,000 people, and in the process of all that fun and frolic, raises $220,000 for charity annually. (What an innovative idea—using garlic as the impetus for a community-wide celebration!)

—**Samuel Evans** had a lifelong dream of leading a marching band. He'd had polio as a child and marching was part of his therapy. So he and his wife Nanette formed their own marching band in 1965 called the Patriots of Northern Virginia. This band now has 450 members (one of the largest marching units in the U.S.) who perform in many of the country's major parades, including the Orange Bowl, Cotton Bowl, Kentucky Derby, 1981 Olympics, 1984 World's Fair, and Macy's Thanksgiving Day Parade. All marchers appear in Colonial garb, which Nanette researches and helps design and sew. Many of the volunteer band members join the band in grade school and stay with it through high school. Mr. Evans has fulfilled his dream and in the process has brought joy to thousands.

—**Bertha Bowles** of the Bronx, New York, loves to entertain people in her home, so she became a volunteer with the International Center. Through her involvement, she has provided temporary homes for more than 3,000 foreign visitors to New York over the past 30 years. Her natural hospitality and enjoyment of all types of people has turned into a lifetime of meeting her own needs as well as the needs of those fortunate enough to have her as their hostess.

(All of these outstanding people and groups have been recipients of either a President's Volunteer Action Award or Citation.)

It is important for each of us to periodically stop and assess both what we have and what we do, and then ask the critical question: Do these possessions and these activities bring joy into my life? If not, the solution may be to share your time and resources with others as a volunteer.

> *The reward, the real grace, of conscious service is the opportunity not only to help relieve suffering but to grow in wisdom, experience greater unity, and have a good time while we're doing it.*[6]

—•2•—

Helping Others
When You're Busy

Your life is busy—but is it full?

—*Apple Computer, Inc.*
Volunteer Program Slogan

For many people today, the desire to help is there—it is finding the *time* to help that is the problem. Two career marriages, professionals with heavy job responsibilities, single parenting, homemakers who have inherited all the neighborhood latch-key youngsters, and retired couples and business people who travel a great deal—all of these societal trends make time a most precious commodity. And yet, when helping others becomes a priority, people in all of those situations have found the time to do it. In fact, two-thirds of today's volunteers are employed either full- or part-time.

In our present society, it is easy to become overwhelmed by the enormity of the challenges we face and feel that one person cannot possibly make a difference. I have found countless stories of individuals and groups across the nation who have discovered how they can fit volunteering into extremely busy lives—*and make a significant difference!* When asked what one person could do for his country, President Teddy Roosevelt replied, "Do whatever you can, wherever you are, with whatever you have!"

You would be astonished at how many people you interact with in the course of your daily life have some type of volunteer involvement that you know nothing about. For example, it was after I began writing this book that I found out:

- My dentist volunteers as host for a ragtime musical program on public radio.

- My hairdresser volunteers as a counselor for a teen alcohol rehabilitation program.

- A friend of mine, who is a masseuse, gives free massages for Hospice patients and their families.

- My dental hygienist has volunteered for three years as a guide and instructor in a nature trail program.

And I'm sure there are many others I'll continue to discover. How wonderful it is that these busy people quietly go about investing precious leisure time in causes they care about. I urge you to have the fun of uncovering the hidden heroes in your circle of business associates, acquaintances, and friends. You'll be surprised, I assure you.

According to the Gallup Survey on volunteering, more than 50 percent of the people who refused to volunteer *when asked* gave "lack of time, too busy" as their primary reason. Unfortunately, the obvious follow-up question was not asked: Too busy doing what? This dilemma is poignantly illustrated by the words of Confucius:

*We are so busy doing the urgent that we do not have
time to do the important.*

Time is Our Most Precious Asset

Life is really made up of choices—and we all make them
every day. That is both the advantage and disadvantage of
being human and having free will. The quality of our lives
is very much determined by the quality of the choices we
make. One of the most difficult decisions we make is how to
use the time we have. The fact is, everyone has the same
amount to work with:

- **24 hours a day**

- **168 hours per week**

- **720 hours per month**

- **8,760 hours per year**

No matter how hard we try, we cannot change that
reality, but we *can* change what we do with the hours we
have. The danger is, in a world moving as fast as ours, it
becomes increasingly easy to confuse the urgent with the
important.

I have too often shared the anguish portrayed in the
following poem by our family friend, Lyman Randall. The
poem is from his book, *Notes from Midlife*:

No Time

*If only I had more time,
I would stop and listen to you.
If only I had more time,
I might try something new.*

*If only I had more time,
I could rest my load awhile.*

If only I had more time,
I might return your smile.

If the day had more hours,
I might get everything done.
And then I could take some time
To enjoy some hard-earned fun.

I hope I have some time
To spend before I die
To figure where my years went
And why I want to cry.

But no time now for tears
Nor any time for prayers
No time to calm my fears
No time
No time
No time![1]

In Thornton Wilder's classic play *Our Town*, Emily, the central character, dies in childbirth. She asks the Stage Manager if she might return home for just one day. Reluctantly, he allows her to do so. She is torn by the beauty of the ordinary and by people's lack of awareness of it. She cries out to her mother, "Mama, just look at me one minute as though you really saw me . . . it goes so fast we don't have time to look at one another." Then she goes back to the cemetery and the quiet company of others lying there, and she asks the Stage Manager, "Do any human beings ever realize life while they live it?" He sighs and says, "No. The saints and poets, maybe. They do some."[2]

Are you realizing life while you're living it? Or are you just going through the motions? Are you running harder and faster to get ahead (or even just to keep up), but feeling little personal fulfillment? Are people as important to you as things, and if so, how much of your time are you devoting to them? Are the people and causes you care most about getting your best time and energy, or only what is left over?

The Danger of Being Too Busy

At one point in my life I experienced a classic case of burnout. It was during this frightening episode that I realized the importance of these questions. When I honestly confronted myself and the choices I was making about the use of my time and energy, I was able to make the changes necessary to regain my health and peace of mind. In my second book, *Survival Skills for Managers*, there is a chapter entitled "Stress Management: Taming the Quiet Killer." In it I share how I felt before and after this experience:[3]

BEFORE	AFTER
Overwhelmed	Centered
Out of control	Values/goals clarified
Loss of energy	Renewed energy
No enthusiasm	Eager
Resentful	Accepting
Distrustful	Trusting
Martyred	Enjoyable to be around
Trouble with words	Productive
Loss of sensory perception	Senses sharp
Loss of humor	Humor returned
Trouble sleeping	Ready for the day
Fatigue	Rested
Annoyed at small things	Calm
Eating/drinking too much	Vigorous
Pain in the neck!	I like me better!

The system I used to overcome my burnout was simple, but painful. I listed the ten things I cared most about in the world and struggled with that list until I could put each item in the order of its priority for me. Then I carefully scrutinized my calendar for the past year to determine where my time had been invested. It became clear that my time and values were out of synch, as 60 percent of my time and most of my energy had gone to the activities that were not highest on my values list. The most important things on my list—my family, my spiritual life, and me—were getting the "leftovers" of my time. No wonder I felt used up. The very activities and people who could renew me were being neglected. It all had to do with choices I had made about use of my time. Once acknowledged, I could determine what I had to stop doing, start doing, and keep doing. It wasn't easy, but it was certainly worth it.

Burnout is a very serious medical and emotional problem. It has been linked to many major illnesses, not just ulcers as was formerly thought. Coping with burnout often means we may need to slow down our hectic pace and make a change in our lifestyle and commitments or move on to a totally new and different challenge. Volunteering can provide that new challenge for some people. It can offer that much-needed safe and neutral space where we can examine values and determine what we want to do next.

A good friend of mine, Sheila Albert, had founded and been executive director of a very successful Volunteer Center for 16 years. She was extremely good at what she did, but was "running too hard and fast," and was beginning to experience many of the burnout symptoms. Finally she decided she needed to make a change of careers. She was able to take some time off between jobs and found that the most renewing thing she did during that time was to become a volunteer for the Audubon Canyon Ranch in northern California:

> At the time I started volunteering for the Audubon Canyon Ranch, I felt like my life was in turmoil! I was trying to find a new direction for my life, and my volunteer experience was incredibly helpful. I was a volunteer

docent at a nature preserve, and took children on hikes to learn about nature. It was phenomenal for me to have a chance to become involved in nature, an interest I had always had, but had never been able to use professionally. And it was such a nourishing thing to do at a time when I *really* needed it. To be surrounded by nature, where everything is so ordered, at a chaotic time in my life was incredibly helpful.

It is important to note, however, that one can burn out as a volunteer as well. I've seen it happen all too frequently. It usually indicates that a person has been in one volunteer position too long, is holding too many volunteer jobs at once, is matched to a wrong assignment, is overwhelmed by the task, or is in need of a sabbatical or "time out" from all unnecessary commitments.

In *The Caring Question*, the authors, Donald and Nancy Tubesing, talk about the essential balance between taking care of ourselves and caring for others: "If you seek wellness by loving and caring for yourself with no regard for your neighbor, you cannot be whole. If you try loving your neighbor without also loving and caring for yourself, God help your neighbor. Neither of you will be whole."[4]

Limited Time—So Many Options

One of the realities of living in an information/service society, as opposed to an agricultural society, is that we have so many options to choose from in all aspects of life, that it often becomes overwhelming. In his book, *Megatrends*, John Naisbitt points out, "Today's a Baskin-Robbins Society, everything comes in 31 flavors." We have:

- **752 different car and truck models**
- **2,500 types of light bulbs**
- **4,000 special interest magazines**

- **200 brands of cigarettes**
- **500,000 self-help groups**
- **13 definitions of 'family'**

So, not only is our time more limited, but our options in all aspects of life have increased—what a dilemma! However, Naisbitt shares this bit of encouragement in the midst of our confusion: "A society can tell it is growing if the options for its citizens are increasing."[5]

Then there are the choices we have to make about causes and needs (if we choose to become involved). Television and newspapers bring them all right into our living rooms every day. In the excellent book *How Can I Help?*, by Ram Dass and Paul Gorman, there is a powerful story about one person's internal struggle between mind and heart and the difficult choices people with limited time need to make:

Sometimes I help, and sometimes I don't.

I hold the door open for one behind me, or I rush through preoccupied in thought. I vote, but not always. When solicitations come through the mail, some catch my eye or heart and I send at least something. Others I basket as junk mail. A friend is having a hard time. I think I should phone to see how she is, but I just don't feel like doing it tonight.

I'd do anything to help the family. But how much is enough? When to stretch a little further? Whose needs come first?

Those close to me get an immediate hearing. The suffering of people more remote gets sporadic attention. I'm only vaguely aware of it. It's out there somewhere.

Whom should I help anyway? Senior citizens, battered children, human-rights victims, whales? Well, if we don't defuse the nuclear threat, there'll be no tomorrow. But if we don't support education and the arts, what kind of tomorrow will it be?

If I stop to think about it, I help out for all kinds of reasons. Maybe it's because I should; it's a matter of responsibility. But there's usually a maze of other motives: a need for self-esteem, approval, status, power; the desire to feel useful, find intimacy, pay back some debt.

Sometimes I'll help through organizations. But the purpose of helping and the people who really need it often seem to fall through the cracks. Maybe I'd rather do it one-to-one, keep my options open, help out here and there.

I expect my government to relieve suffering. Sometimes it does. But it also pays farmers not to produce wheat while somewhere, every forty-five seconds, a small child starves to death. And a public official, no better or worse a person than I, finds reason to justify this policy—but would probably do everything he could, faced with one starving child.

There are times when service is effortless. Other days, burnout. With one person, I'm totally open and present. With the next, I might as well be on Mars. Sometimes the chance to care for another human being feels like such grace. But later on, I'll hear myself thinking, "Hey, what about me?"

Over Gandhi's tomb are inscribed words that say: Think of the poorest person you have ever seen and ask if your next act will be of any use to him. That'll flash through my mind as I prepare to throw a Frisbee. And when I spend fifteen bucks dining out and going to a movie to ward off boredom, I might recall that a fifteen-dollar operation could restore someone's sight in a third-world country. I'm moved by the power of Gandhi's invitation, "Live simply that others might simply live." But I'm not at all clear about how to heed that, day in and day out, here in the affluent West. Sometimes I feel a little guilty.

I'm fortunate, for the moment, to have good health and loving friends, to be housed and fed, with work to do and some time to play. When I myself need help, there's usually someone to call. I'm able to spend some time away from places where suffering is really visible and just can't be screened out.

Yet there are few days when I'm not feeling human pain, my own or another's. If it's not there in front of me, I see a steady stream of images of misery on the evening news of a suffering planet: homeless one huddled by a doorway or tree; old one looking vacant in a nursing home; slain revolutionary or national guardsman, both teen-agers; drunk driver just realizing he's killed his whole family; starving child's bloated belly and haunted eyes; victims of natural disasters; helpless leaders, helpless helpers.

Some images I ponder; what's that one saying? Others make me uneasy; I tune them out. Some make me angry; I want to get up and do something. Others make me sigh; horror and compassion. And finally I might have to turn away, close off, and escape into some philosophical sanctuary. It's all just too much.

How can I keep my heart open and not go under? I've got my own life to live, after all. Still, I'd like to do more for others. What do I have to offer, and what would help most? Complicated business, all this.

Look, you do the best you can . . . [6]

The late Jim Henson, the creative genius who developed "The Muppet Show" and several movies that earned him Emmy, Grammy, and Peabody awards, once made these comments about his choices regarding the use of his time:

> At some point in my life, I decided, rightly or wrongly so, that there are many situations I can't do much about; acts of terrorism, feelings of nationalistic prejudice, and Cold War, etc. What I try to do is concentrate on the situations that my energies can affect . . . When I was young, my ambition was to be one of the people who makes a difference in this world. My hope still is to leave this world a little bit better for my being here. It's a wonderful life and I love it.[7]

How Busy People Are Helping

There are thousands of examples of busy people who find time to volunteer. Many of them can only give an hour or two a week (equivalent to watching one television show), or work on short-term projects, but their efforts are making a tremendous difference in their own lives and in the lives of others. Let me share just a few examples:

—**Suzette Brooks**, a 29-year-old Harvard Law School graduate who now works as a corporate lawyer on Park Avenue, started *New York Cares*. This is a volunteer organization that schedules around the hectic work styles of hundreds of young professionals. "There are a lot of young professionals out there who feel they are focusing much too much on themselves, their career advancement and on their clients," Brooks says. "They want to give something . . . for most of our members it couldn't be more than once a week, simply because of their heavy job commitment." This group of young bankers, lawyers, and junior executives now numbers over 600. They volunteer in a soup kitchen, several homeless shelters and welfare hotels, work with a program for the elderly, and with 38 other volunteer and social service agencies in New York. Brooks says that when she got out of Harvard Law School she had the feeling that it might be time to put something back into the world that was her oyster. "I think a lot of young people realize it might be okay to do a little something more with our lives, even if it means making vice president in two years instead of six months."[8]

—**Jim Huff** is one of 4,000 volunteers around the country who reads books at one of the 31 studios of Recording for the Blind. He's been doing this once a week for almost 15 years. Huff is an engineering staff specialist with a division of General Dynamics. He uses his technical skill in his volunteer work, as he translates complex mathematical and technical data into an understandable audiotape. He makes an invaluable contribution with his two hours per week because almost 60 percent of the tens of thousands of books requested from Recording for the Blind during the 1987-88 school year were technical, a 40 percent increase since 1972. Huff says, "I would think that being blind while trying to get a college education is going to be a handicap, all right. If those kids are willing to put the work in . . . I'll help 'em a little bit."[9]

—**Bud Struble** works the first shift at the Cessna Aircraft Company and a "second shift" refurbishing toys for needy children in Harper County, Kansas. He rescues discarded tricycles, wagons, and other toys, and makes them look like new by working on them at night in his barn. Struble says his volunteer work "sure makes you feel good."[10]

—**LTV Aircraft Products employees** in Texas gave an estimated 15,000 hours of volunteer service in 1988. Two examples of their projects: collecting 700,000 pounds of food for the North Texas Food Bank (equaling more than *one million meals*), and working for the tenth year at an inner-city elementary school in the Reading-is-Fundamental program.

LTV volunteers read to students; discuss current events; and help with science fairs, spelling bees, and field days.

—**The National Association of Letter Carriers** found a way to help others during their regular duties of delivering mail. Carrier Alert is a project in which letter carriers watch for indications of trouble on their regular routes—such as accumulated mail and newspapers at the residences of elderly, disabled, and homebound patrons. Their vigilance has been responsible for saving numerous lives since it was begun in 1982. In 1985, they added Child Watch, and stay on the alert for missing children whose photographs appear in their monthly union magazine. This project was a 1986 President's Volunteer Action Award winner.

—**Brandon Johnson**, a Washington D.C. attorney, has spent one or two nights a week for the past six years volunteering at an adult literacy center on Capitol Hill. "I don't have any training in teaching," he says. "I just found I enjoyed it . . . it's a fantastic feeling when they start to learn." He also volunteers with an organization called Concerned Black Men which was formed several years ago to build positive male role models for children. "African Americans need to do more to help their own people. I hope my being a volunteer will make others see the need. It's not a matter of finding time, it's *making* time."[11]

There are thousands of examples of individuals and groups who are making time to volunteer, either through their work or after work. In fact, according to a July 10, 1989, *Newsweek* article, the number of companies that send workers into community service has doubled to an estimated 1,200 since 1984.

It Takes So Little to Make a Difference

One of the dangers of our "bigger is better" society is that it becomes easy to overlook how important seemingly small acts of kindness and caring can be. Someone once said, "A few kind words take only seconds to say, but their echoes go on for years." No matter how busy we are, we all have time for this!

This quotation reminded me of a story about Ashley Montagu that I read in the book, *The Courage of Conviction*. During the 1940s and '50s he was perhaps the best known anthropologist and one of the most popular university professors in the United States. He told about being a lonely, only child in England who found the world open up to him through the world of books. By the age of 10, he had acquired an insatiable interest and curiosity about human behavior, the brain, and eventually anthropology. When he was 15, a friend's father gave him a human skull to study. This is what he did with it:

> I mustered up enough courage to take the skull, in a brown paper bag, to the Royal College of Surgeons, where I knew the world's most famous physical anthropologist, Sir Arthur Keith, was conservator. Arriving at the imposing building, I was met in the portico by an even more imposing dignitary, a man in a blue, brass-buttoned uniform, who appeared at least nine feet tall . . . I said I would like to see Sir Arthur Keith. He further inquired for what purpose. Whereupon I told him what I had in the brown paper bag, and that I would like Sir Arthur to explain its mysteries to me. Whereupon my genial porter retired and soon returned accompanied by a tall, benevolent, handsome man in his early fifties. Clad in his white lab coat, this was Sir Arthur Keith, who, putting his arm round my shoulders, gently guided me into his laboratory, seated me, and treated me as if I were a learned colleague of not less status than himself. After explaining the skull to me . . . Sir Arthur asked me about myself, and then extended to me the invitation to come and take advantage of the . . . anatomical and anthropological materials over which he presided.

It can well be imagined what an effect this great man's civility to a young boy had. It is an effect that has had a tremendous influence upon me, especially in my relations with children and students.[12]

And since Dr. Montagu later taught at New York University, Rutgers University, the University of California at Santa Barbara, and Princeton University—this one act of kindness on the part of a very busy person was multiplied a thousand-fold.

Perhaps one of the greatest lessons a person can learn is that very often the most meaningful gift you can give to another person is to just be there, fully present to them. That doesn't take a large investment of time, but it can make a tremendous difference to others.

I have discussed this with my dear friend Warren, who is a pastor. For the first 20 years of his ministry, Warren was a real go-getter. His energy, enthusiasm, and creativity ensured that every congregation he served grew and flourished dramatically. And then, at age 50, he had a very serious stroke and lost the ability to walk, talk, and read. After many months of intensive rehabilitation and dogged determination, he recovered most of his faculties to the point where he is again serving his congregation as full-time pastor. Warren commented on how differently he views his ministry now: "I used to dislike hospital calls and would hurry through them so that I could get on with the important stuff," he says. "Now, I realize they are the important stuff! I may just sit quietly with a person for 30 minutes or an hour—just being there."

There are thousands of examples of small acts of caring that are so meaningful to others. Here are a few examples that come to mind:

—When I was the director of the Boulder County Volunteer and Information Center in Boulder, Colorado, some of our retired senior volunteers worked on used dolls we collected at the center for the holiday Share-a-Gift program. These volunteers would clean them, reattach limbs, untangle and curl hair (or fit them with wigs), and even knit or sew new clothes for the dolls. By Christmas Eve, dozens of little girls had good-as-new dolls under their trees.

—A friend of mine, who plays ragtime and "golden oldies" on the piano, plays at two different nursing homes twice a month for patient sing-along sessions. They love it and so does she.

—My family participates in the welfare department's Adopt-a-Family program during the holidays. We are given the first names, ages, and want/wish lists of each member of a welfare family. Then we have a family outing to buy the gifts and each take part in wrapping and labeling each one. It's a very special part of our holidays.

—A retired bus driver in Denver, Colorado, has become a one-man welcoming committee for new arrivals at Denver's downtown bus terminal. He keeps his eyes open for elderly riders who often become confused by a big city terminal and also for youngsters who are often prey for unsavory characters. He offers a cheerful welcome, advice, directions, information about the city, or any other help needed.

In today's busy world, with so many options and so many demands on our limited time, it *is* possible to help and to make a significant difference in the lives of others. It's simply a matter of deciding what you can give—and then giving it. Remember, volunteering is one activity where a little goes a very long way.

One of the most highly admired and respected people of this century is Mother Teresa, who received the Nobel Peace

Prize in 1979 for her work with the poorest of the poor in India. Wherever she goes in her travels around the world, people inevitably ask her, What can I do to help? In her lovely book, *Words to Love By*, she shares her answer:

> *Just begin, one, one, one. Begin at home by saying something good to your child, to your husband or to your wife. Begin by helping someone in need in your community, at work, or at school. Begin by making whatever you do something beautiful for God . . .*

> *I never look at the masses as my responsibility. I look at the individual. I can love only one person at a time. I can feed only one person at a time. Just one, one, one . . . I picked up one person—maybe if I didn't pick up that one person I wouldn't have picked up 42,000. The whole work is only a drop in the ocean. But if I didn't put the drop in, the ocean would be one drop less.*

> *Same thing for you.*
> *Same thing for your family.*
> *Same thing in the church where you go.*
> *Just begin . . . one, one, one.*[13]

—•3•—

Reaching Out When You're Lonely or in Transition

When we break through and meet in spirit behind our separateness, we experience profound moments of companionship. These, in turn, give us access to deeper and deeper levels of generosity and loving kindness. True compassion arises out of unity. All the more painful, then, are the moments in which we feel cut off from one another, when we reach out to help or be helped and don't quite meet.

—Ram Dass and Paul Gorman

It is often during life's major transitions such as loss of a loved one, moving to a new community, loss of a job, or divorce, that we experience the greatest loneliness. During these times, volunteering can be a very helpful and healing experience—because it is in the reaching out to others that we are able to "get out" of ourselves.

However, for many people the greatest block to volunteering at times like these is lack of confidence or self-esteem. They may honestly question whether they have anything of value to share with others.

These feelings of loneliness and isolation are poignantly expressed in this poem by Lyman Randall:

Loneliness

Loneliness surrounds me
Pushing me inside,
Keeping me apart
From the flow of faces,
The people passing.

I feel like calling out,
"Hey! Here I am!
You don't know what you're missing,
Not knowing me."

Untuned ears
On unturned heads
Ignore me.

I reach out,
Searching for a human touch.
Into my hand falls a coin, a tear,
Then another hand, clutching.
I wrench free.

Is the field full of touch-me-nots
Or is it me who is afraid
To touch another?
What is it that I must give
Of me to get from another
That for which I search?
The only gift that I can give
Is Me.

(The thought makes me tremble.)

What if it is not enough?
To give but not be taken
Erases the soul.

Loneliness surrounds me
Still pushing me inside
But from my empty prison
To others outside I shout:
"Hey! Let me in!"
They answer:
"But you were never out."[1]

Risking to Reach Out

According to the Gallup Survey on volunteering, 40 percent of the people who volunteer were personally asked to become involved. Only 19 percent sought out the activity on their own. But an amazing 74 percent of those who were asked said yes to the request. These responses show that Americans are very willing to volunteer *when asked.*

I suspect that one of the reasons it is difficult for many people to look for ways to share their time and talents as volunteers is the fear of seeming too bold or pushy. Many of us have been taught that humility is a virtue, and sometimes this can make reaching out to help difficult.

I remember when I was growing up, we were taught in Sunday School not to be boastful. That was drummed into us so much that when it came time in later years to volunteer my talents, I had to work through some internal reluctance to tell others what I was good at. One time I had an opportunity to do some training at my own church. It went very well and I loved doing it. Afterwards, one of the church "pillars" came up to me and with a slight frown said, "That really turned you on, didn't it Marlene?" I immediately felt the rush of old guilt and it took a few minutes before I recovered enough to say, "Yes, it did. It felt so good to finally be asked to do what I do best for my own church!"

In his book *Markings,* Dag Hammarskjold had this to say about humility:

> Humility is just as much the opposite of self-abasement as it is of self-exaltation. To be humble is *not to make comparisons.* Secure in its reality, the self is neither better nor worse, bigger nor smaller, than anything else in the universe. It *is*—is nothing, yet at the same time one with everything. It is in this sense that humility is absolute self-effacement.

> . . . To give to people, works, poetry, art, what the self can contribute, and to take, simply and freely, what belongs to it by reason of its identity. Praise and blame, the winds of success and adversity, blow over such a life without leaving a trace or upsetting its balance . . .[2]

I believe we have been given our unique and individual gifts, talents, and abilities to share with others. We all should feel more comfortable about celebrating our talents, and enjoy using them fully.

Another stumbling block for many people in trying to become involved when they are lonely or in transition is that their self-esteem is low, their energy is drained, and they are afraid to risk reaching out to others. This dilemma is illustrated so well in this passage from the book *Living, Loving & Learning,* by Leo Buscaglia:

> *To laugh is to risk appearing the fool.*
> *To weep is to risk being called sentimental.*
> *To reach out to another is to risk involvement.*
> *To expose feelings is to risk showing your true self.*
> *To place your ideas and your dreams before the crowd*
>   *is to risk being called naive.*
> *To love is to risk not being loved in return.*
> *To live is to risk dying.*

To hope is to risk despair and to try is to risk failure.

But risks must be taken, because the greatest risk in life is to risk nothing. The person who risks nothing, does nothing, has nothing, is nothing and becomes nothing. He may avoid suffering and sorrow, but he simply cannot learn and feel and change and grow and love and live. Chained by his certitudes, he's a slave. He's forfeited his freedom. Only the person who risks is truly free.[3]

If you are lonely or in transition, and your goal is to have a fuller, richer life, then risking is a necessary part of that journey. And reaching out to others in the safe and caring environment of a volunteer organization is a good way to begin.

Loss of a Loved One

When I was director of the Boulder Volunteer and Information Center, a woman came in one day in response to an article about our center and our work of matching volunteers to needs in the community. She said she really didn't know if volunteering was the answer for her, but she was desperately lonely and was willing to do something if we could find a place for her. When I asked her what she would like to do, she said, "take care of sick people." Then she shared with me that she had devoted the last 14 years to caring for her husband who had been an invalid. Since he had died a few weeks before, she felt totally lost and unneeded. She said she'd like to care for sick people "because that's all I know how to do."

It took some gentle prodding on my part to get her to admit that taking care of sick people was probably not what she *needed* to do at that time. During our conversation, I discovered that she really enjoyed her grandchildren (and she shyly admitted they liked her too), but she didn't get to see them often because they lived in another state. I ended up referring her to a volunteer job tutoring three little boys in reading at a school near her home. It was love at first sight—for all of them. She enjoyed it so much that she was soon doing other volunteer work for the school and eventually branched out to other community agencies. She became so busy I had trouble catching her at home!

When the death of a loved one is a violent death, then the loss is often even more difficult to deal with because of the anger and hostility felt by loved ones, as this story illustrates:

> After an escaped convict shot and killed her 24-year-old son, Lois Hess considered smuggling a gun into court and shooting him. Instead, she turned grief into belief. Since that day in 1975, Hess, 61, has battled endlessly and effectively for gun control—testifying, writing, fund raising. Her lobbying was one reason Maryland's electorate voted to ban the sale of cheap handguns last year. "It's rewarding to know that maybe I'm helping save one life," she says. "One life would be worth all the trouble I've been through."[4]

Perhaps one of the best-known stories of grief redirected to positive action is how Candy Lightner founded MADD (Mothers Against Drunk Driving) after her daughter, Cari, was killed by a drunk driver. "It was the second time that my daughter had been hit by a drunk driver," she stated, "and finally it had cost her life. Also I had two other children that I was very concerned about, so I had a paranoid fear, and also I was very angry and bitter. And yes, I was thinking revenge . . . I wanted the man who killed my daughter punished." Her efforts gained national attention, and from the first meager beginnings of the organization in Candy's den, MADD now has over 300 chapters and more than 600,000 donors and volunteers. Liquor consumption has dropped nationally and laws against drunk driving are much tougher.[5] (This is an inspirational example of what can happen when the energy caused by grief can be redirected outward instead of inward.)

As I mentioned in the preface, I lost my husband, Harvey, in July 1989. Although it was a sudden, violent death, (he was struck by a truck and was killed instantly) it was quite different from the experiences of either Lois Hess or Candy Lightner. The driver was not drinking, on drugs, or exceeding the speed limit. Harvey had stopped by the road to enjoy his favorite hobby, photography, and when he crossed the road, he neglected to look both ways. This loss of a loved one is as painful, but is different in that there is immense sadness instead of anger or bitterness. What place has volunteering had in the healing process for me and our two young adult children, Richard and Lisa? We have spent hours talking about the importance of reaching out to others, and our committment to carrying on the spirit of giving and helpfulness to others that epitomized Harvey's life. Part of our healing journey has been and will continue to be to discover and invest our energies in those causes that we feel can truly make this world a better place for generations to come.

The following is a eulogy which one of Harvey's dear friends, Pat Westerhouse, wrote and shared at Harvey's funeral. It offers a valuable message about the importance of reaching out when grieving the loss of a loved one:

> *Take your moment to mourn, but don't spend too much time. My life was a wonderful celebration. I am still with you and love you, but now you must seek me in different ways. Learn to:*
>
> *See my face in the beauty of the world and hear my laughter in the giggle of a small child. Feel my touch in the warmth of the sun, and my voice in the gentle stirring of the wind, and most of all, know I am present to you always in the quiet strength of our love for each other.*

If you feel burdened with the problems of the day, or fear the uncertainty of the future, seek me in the wisdom and counsel of family and friends. If you feel the pain of loneliness or the hurt of separation, reach out to someone else in need of love, for that is how you will quiet your sorrow. And if you seek peace for yourself, listen quietly to the sound of my voice present in your own heart, for that is where I am always.

Were not our lives together more joy than sorrow; more laughter than tears; more forgiveness than separation? So, too, let this experience of life be turned from grief and sadness to one of knowing and seeking the loving God within us all.

When you choose to remember our time together, remember the days of celebration and laughter. In this way the gift of my life and the power of its love will continue to echo in the lives of all you touch.

Moving to a New Community

America is becoming a very mobile society, due primarily to the economic changes we have experienced. It is now a rarity to remain in the same community throughout one's life. So the transition of moving is one most of us have to learn how to accept. Some manage this much more creatively than others. These people frequently attribute their successful transition to becoming actively involved in their new community as quickly as possible.

I have a friend, Sue Vineyard, who learned this lesson as a child. Her father was a salesman for a large national company, and throughout her youth they moved over a dozen times. This can be devastating to a child, but Sue learned that she could be accepted and become part of a group more quickly by sharing her talent in art. Whenever posters needed to be done, decorations for parties needed designing, or sets for plays needed painting—she volunteered to help. These involvements led to friendships, and soon she was no longer an outsider.

Research has shown that it is best to get new people actively involved within the first three months of joining any type of membership organization. The major reason is that people are eager to find a place to belong and feel accepted, and will search until they find it, especially when they are new to a community.

One of my favorite examples of how volunteering can help a person find a meaningful place after moving (and achieve personal growth at the same time) is the story of Mary, one of our first volunteers at the Boulder Volunteer and Information Center.

Mary was in her mid-forties, newly divorced, financially well-to-do, and had just moved to our community. The only person she knew in town was her real estate agent, who suggested she might want to visit our center since she was feeling very lonely and unsure. She wanted and needed to have something to do and a way to meet people.

As I interviewed her, I discovered she'd been a secretary 20 years ago so I asked her if she'd like to do some typing for us. She wanted to start immediately, which pleased us, as we really needed the help. After she typed her first few letters, a slight problem became apparent—the letters were riddled with errors (she hadn't typed much for 20 years). Suppressing my first impulse, which was to have my secretary correct the letters after Mary left, I asked Mary if she had time to re-do them. She laughed and admitted she'd forgotten she was supposed to proofread, and stayed until the letters were perfect. She immediately enrolled in an evening typing class and in no time her secretarial skills were first rate.

Mary loved our center—it was the hub of community activity—and she worked with us several days a week. She eventually learned to interview volunteers; answer information calls; and recruit, screen, and schedule all of the office volunteers. After several years she left and became the director of Big Sisters in Boulder. I believe that Mary was one of those people just "waiting to happen"—and volunteering provided her that opportunity.

Loss of a Job

An inevitable result of the enormous changes that have occurred as we have moved from being an industrial society to an information/service society is casualties in the work place. With whole industries closing, down-sizing, or moving to new locations, many American families are dealing first-hand with the problems of loss of jobs, lay offs, and early retirement. And it is affecting both blue- and white-collar workers.

Unfortunately, our culture too often values people for what they do (and how much money they make doing it), instead of who they are. This creates a serious self-esteem crisis for many people. One of the great challenges we face today is to help people learn that they can achieve meaning and self-worth, as well as new skills and motivation, through meaningful volunteer work. Winston Churchill wisely observed, "We make a living by what we get, but we make a life by what we give!"

One of the challenges is that many of those affected by these changes are men, especially in their fifties and sixties, and many in this group often hold the opinion that volunteering is "women's work." We found this to be true in our Boulder community a few years ago when we started a Senior Involvement Volunteer Task Force and tried to recruit older men. This became a priority for us when we learned from our county's Department of Employment that a shocking number of retired men die in the first three years after retirement. As the director said, "They no longer have a reason to get up!"

But finding appropriate projects to appeal to these men took some creativity. One of the most popular was a program run by the city to provide repairs and winterization of houses owned by low income elderly people. The city was planning to recruit university students as volunteers for the program. We convinced them, however, that these retired men had been fixing up their own houses for years and that the older home owners would probably be more comfortable letting them into their homes. It was a wonderful success. Since the men worked in teams, socialization needs were met as well. After that, more and more retired men in the community broadened their concept of volunteering and joined the women in responding to hundreds of needs over the next few years. The Boulder Volunteer and Information Center eventually wrote a grant for a Retired Senior Volunteer Program (RSVP) and in its first 10 years, more than 1,200 seniors volunteered through RSVP in Boulder County.

There are several examples of outstanding volunteer contributions by individual retirees in chapter 7.

In Barberton, Ohio, the Barberton Council of Labor faced a critical community problem after several plants closed in the county. The unemployment rate was 33 percent. Many unemployed persons lost not just their jobs, but their health insurance as well. So the Council decided to set up a free medical clinic. The Council donated their building in 1984, and in 1988, they were able to move to a larger facility donated by the Ohio Brass Union, which was extensively remodeled by Council member volunteers and craft union members. Hospitals and doctors donated equipment and churches, business, and unions donated money for supplies.

This clinic now serves approximately 1,300 people a year and is staffed by more than 100 volunteers. Besides many professional volunteers (i.e. doctors, nurses, medical students, social workers), many of the volunteers are the unemployed persons who also receive services. They receive training, job experience, and an improved sense of self-worth and community involvement. This program deservedly won a President's Volunteer Action Award in 1988.

Newly Single

To be newly single through divorce or death of a spouse often creates a serious sense of loneliness or isolation for many people. Social functions and groups are often designed for couples and the single person can feel like an unwelcome outsider. This may also be true when a single person moves to a new community, leaving old friends, family, and other support systems behind. It can be a wrenching situation for the newly divorced or widowed person, whose former circle of friends was most likely couples. Now he or she doesn't seem to fit in, and no one quite knows what to do for them or with them.

The problem for many is meeting new people and connecting with others who share their values. More and more are rejecting the singles bars, dating services, and personal ads but are still searching for alternatives.

One innovative program designed to meet this growing need was started in Jacksonville, Florida, in 1986. It's called the Upbeat program and is sponsored by the city's Volunteer Center. The idea came from the center's director, Sarah Monroe, and a group of nine of her single friends. Sarah had experienced the problem personally when she went through a divorce in mid-life. She and her friends were discussing the dilemma one day and decided to each invite 10 more singles to a brainstorming meeting. (This was not hard to do, since 40 percent of Jacksonville's population is single.)

The idea they had was to combine the need of single adults to meet one another, with the desire to do something worthwhile for the community. As the original group discussed the idea, great enthusiasm was generated and the Upbeat program was born.

To belong, volunteers must attend at least half of Upbeat's monthly meetings and participate in a minimum of four of the group's volunteer projects a year. Volunteers range in age from 20 to 60. The group has grown so rapidly that recruitment is now only through word of mouth rather than actively publicizing the program. Members love being together, doing worthwhile projects, and making lasting friendships in the process.

Typical of the projects undertaken by Upbeat volunteers are: painting a day care center, working with Special Olympics children, ushering at the Florida Theatre, taking part in community fund raisers such as the spring music festival, participating in YMCA's fitness festival, serving as marshals at the Gator Bowl parade, and organizing a picnic outing for nursing home residents.[6]

This is one of those wonderful, innovative ideas that can easily be duplicated in any community. To help this happen, Volunteer Jacksonville has published a simple manual on how they organized their program. To order "How to Develop a Volunteer Program for Single Adults," write to Volunteer Jacksonville, 1600 Prudential Drive, Jacksonville, Florida 32207, or call (904) 398-7777.

If you are lonely or experiencing a major transition in your life, the following suggestions from the excellent book *The Caring Question*, by Donald and Nancy Tubesing, might help you start to reach out to others.[7]

26 OUTREACH OPTIONS

1. Be a foster grandparent

2. Counsel at a camp for handicapped kids

3. Provide a listening ear for Hospice patients

4. Act as chauffeur for kids with working parents

5. Share your talents and knowledge with nursing home residents

6. Invite a foreign student to spend time with your family

7. Sit with a stranger in church and listen empathetically afterwards

 8. Pick up group-home residents to share in a family outing

 9. Visit regularly at a jail or prison

10. Find a job for a refugee

11. Deliver meals on wheels

12. Donate blood regularly

13. Supervise the playground during lunch periods

14. Adopt a grandparent in your neighborhood

15. Assist with health screenings

16. Relieve parents of a chronically-ill child

17. Stop for a stranded motorist

18. Take a loaf of bread to a bereaved neighbor, even if you don't know her well

19. Open your home to victims of a disaster

20. Fund a week at camp for a needy child

21. Talk to the shopping-bag lady outside the library

22. Support your local Boys' Club or Girl Scouts with time as well as money

23. Telephone someone you know is lonely

24. Transport seniors to the store or appointments

25. Give back rubs at a day-care center

26. Write cards and letters frequently to folks who need their spirits lifted.

In the book *Is It Worth Dying For?*, the authors talk about the difference between the Red Sea and the Dead Sea in the Middle East. The Red Sea, which is fed by several tributaries and empties into several others, has some of the most beautiful, sparkling, life-sustaining water in the world. The Dead

Sea, on the other hand, is locked into itself and can neither give nor sustain life. Their conclusion: "Giving is getting. . . don't dam yourself up. Let your water flow."[8]

The Call

Throughout your life, there is a voice only you can hear. A voice which mythologists label "the call." A call to the value of your own life. The choice of risk and individual bliss over the known and secure.

You may choose not to hear your spirit. You may prefer to build a life within the compound, to avoid risk. It is possible to find happiness within a familiar box, a life of comfort and control.

Or, you may choose to be open to new experiences, to leave the limits of your conditioning, to hear the call. Then you must act.

If you never hear it perhaps nothing is lost. If you hear it and ignore it, your life is lost.[9]

—•4•—

Learning and Growing Through Sharing

Growth has not only rewards and pleasure but also many intrinsic pains and always will have. Each step forward is a step into the unfamiliar and is possibly dangerous. It also means giving up something familiar and good and satisfying. It frequently means a parting and a separation, even a kind of death prior to rebirth, with consequent nostalgia, fear, loneliness and mourning. It also means giving up a simpler and easier and less effortful life, in exchange for a more demanding, more responsible, more difficult life . . . it therefore requires courage, will, choice and strength in the individual, as well as protection, permission and encouragement from the environment.[1]

—Abraham Maslow

We each make decisions about how we will use our time every day of our lives, but I fear that these day-to-day choices often take up so much time and energy that it's easy to evade or miss the larger question: *What do I envision as the central purpose or mission of my life?* When we deal with that question, the everyday decisions are made in the context of this larger goal. When we do not have a larger vision for our lives, the day-to-day choices take us somewhere by default. But is that where we really want to be? We often bemoan how much time people waste. I believe the greater tragedy is how many lives are wasted.

Our Attitudes Affect Our Growth

There is nothing that affects our goals, actions, and impact on others more dramatically than our attitudes. We've all heard the simplistic but true portrayal of the difference between those who say a cup is half empty and those who see it as half full. They are called pessimists and optimists. We discover how dramatically attitudes vary as we deal with this subject of learning and growing. Some examples are:

> *"I now have been in this field long enough to finally know what some of the questions are . . . how exciting it will be to discover a few answers and many more questions."*

> *"Learning's for kids—why should I go back to school at my age?"*

> *"Don't confuse me with facts!"*

> *"Education is a reorganization of what you may already know."*

> *"You go to school to be able to get a job that pays well. Don't expect to find one you like —that's not realistic or practical."*

"Life is a journey, not a destination."

"There's so much to learn, I can't wait to retire to have more time to explore those things I've always wondered about."

"Learning's a drag!"

"Learning's fun!"

And the list could go on and on. Neither volunteering nor any other activity will provide an opportunity for learning and growing unless a person has an attitude that allows it to happen.

I knew two people from the corporate world who volunteered for the board of directors of the same agency. One plunged into the job with enthusiasm and eagerly did her homework before each board meeting. She wanted to learn as much as possible about the differences between a corporation and a nonprofit agency. She became very committed to the mission of the agency, which provided quality health care for indigent clients. She often volunteered at the agency's clinic so she could understand the needs of the clients and make more informed decisions at the board meetings. Her corporate colleague, on the other hand, came to the task of board member with a somewhat arrogant opinion that he knew more than the agency staff and therefore his role was to teach instead of learn. He rarely read the materials sent before the meetings, and frequently left the meetings early. He found the commitment tiresome and resigned before his term ended.

These predictable outcomes are often called self-fulfilling prophecies, or getting back what you give out.

Each human being is a process—a filtering process of retention or rejection, absorption or loss. The

*process defines individuality. It determines whether
we justify the gift of human life or whether we live
and die without having been affected by the beauty
of wonder and the wonder of beauty, without
having had any real awareness of kinship or human
fulfillment.*

—*Norman Cousins*

Developing New Skills

In chapter 3, I discussed the Senior Involvement Volunteer Task Force we established at the Volunteer and Information Center in Boulder. The remarkable woman who helped us start this program was named Clara. She was married to a retired Army officer and had lived all over the world. She had several children, so throughout her life had volunteered extensively in their activities, as well as in the various Army communities where they had lived.

When she came to the center, her husband had retired, the kids were grown and on their own, and Clara was looking for a challenge. She saw herself as a good "worker bee," but had reservations about her leadership abilities. I saw in her someone who was dedicated to the needs of seniors, knowledgeable about our community, an idea person, and a real go-getter, so I convinced her to become the first chairperson of the task force.

I strongly believed my role as agency director was one of enabling our key volunteer leaders to succeed, so I set about helping her get the money, agency support, volunteer staff, and transportation she needed to implement her excellent ideas. When she began to see her ideas flourish, she became more and more confident. She began to see herself, not just as a doer of someone else's programs, but as an innovative leader. It was under her leadership that the senior volunteer program grew from 10 seniors to 350 in less than 3 years.

"That was the best time of my life," she says. "I finally got a chance to discover what I could really do and then do it!"

Volunteering can also provide you the opportunity to work in new areas that interest you professionally. In the April 24, 1989 issue of *U.S. News and World Report*, there was an article by Terri Thompson and Sharon Golden about volunteering to discover a new career:

> When a career goes stale, volunteerism can help you find a new one . . . Most volunteer groups would like to take advantage of volunteers' existing skills but are usually quite willing to let them try out new areas too. A lawyer who wants to try her hand at public relations, for instance, will be able to do just that. Latent talents in selling and marketing might be unearthed through jobs that involve you with fund raising. Helping plan innovative methods of producing income may bring out the entrepreneur in you. You can learn about the inner workings of government by lobbying legislators for an environmental group, perhaps leading to a paying position as lobbyist. By directing volunteers, you may become expert in counseling, administration, personnel management, and recruitment.[2]

As this article points out, one of the tremendous benefits of volunteering is having the opportunity to work in new areas of interest and decide if it may be a possible new career or vocation for you (paid or volunteer). Experts say that people in this new decade will change careers at least every five years. And since we're living so much longer, that could mean as many as 10 careers in a lifetime—how exciting!

Learning About Other Cultures

Community involvement can also provide the opportunity to learn more about other cultures.

A dear friend of mine, Jane Justis, came from a very traditional, high achievement and success-oriented family. She had the education and personality to choose almost any "fast track" route she wanted as a career. She decided instead to work for an international health organization that saved dying children around the world. As she dealt with the realities of poverty and death, both in rural America and in other nations, Jane learned things about compassion, caring, and priorities that no textbook could ever teach. Let me share with you her own vivid account of one such incident:

I saw the man hurrying down the hall with the bundle in his outstretched hands. I knew by his walk that this was an emergency. As he hurried by, the staring eyes looked back at me. His tiny mouth was open but silent— A cry, but not a cry. Is this one of those times? Are we all to witness one of those "too late" situations? Oh, God, I hope not.

Trailing behind was Mother: nervous, frightened, and crying in a controlled sort of way. She seemed so willing to stand back as they whisked her half-alive son down the hall. Instinctively I looked for the comforters who must be there with her, but she was alone—so alone.

I watched as efficient hands worked to fuse the little human to the life-saving juices from the IV bottle. As I watched, my thoughts turned to the Mother in the hall. I'm so aggressive and impatient. How could she *wait* in the hall? When I saw her, she was leaning against the door, weeping softly and sighing. A distraught and frightened mother. Different language and culture couldn't disguise that.

Oh, how I hurt for her—I love my son so! What could I give her to ease her pain? My gift was a pink Kleenex. I felt so distant as I handed it to her, but I sensed her need to be close—or was it my own need? The tears finally flowed freely—hers and mine. How we held on to each other! A union of two mothers, each wondering why life must be this way.

Two more gifts I gave to that Mother—a chair and a glass of water. But I couldn't give her son. Only God can do that, now. For a moment, time stopped, and the world's rules didn't matter. Two souls jumped infinite boundaries and grieved together. And for that instant we were one.

Another friend of our family, Tom Wimber, was a Peace Corps volunteer in Lesotho, Africa, for four years. Here is what he had to say about his remarkable learning experiences as a volunteer in a different culture:

I taught high school students in the south of Lesotho. After three years of volunteer service plus another year as associate director, I feel pretty much in tune with what the Peace Corps is and does. It is the largest non-military overseas operation in American history. First established by President John F. Kennedy, the Peace Corps was inaugurated on August 30, 1961 when volunteers left for Ghana to teach in secondary schools. Since then, over 120,000 Americans have spent two or more years overseas in 92 nations working to "help people help themselves." Peace Corps arrived in Lesotho in 1967. One of its goals is to provide trained manpower to interested countries. However, its more worthy goal and one which was very evident, is the communion of cultures, and the promotion of understanding between different peoples. Long after my teachings are forgotten, I know my students will remember me as an American and as a good person to know—no matter what my nationality. That is what Peace Corps does best: it brings cultures together.

In many languages of the world, the word for "stranger" is the same as that for "enemy." One of the most distinctive ways Peace Corps volunteers remove that "stranger" stereotype is their ability to speak the local language. Besides the technical training that volunteers receive, language training is heavily stressed—and for good reason. It breaks down the barriers of unfamiliarity and actually impresses the local people.

On the other hand, American volunteers have a lot to learn about their host country. It is a common fact that most volunteers feel that no matter how much technical instruction they may have delivered or how many people they may have influenced, they received far more than they gave. Volunteers are outnumbered, and if they choose to, can become as immersed in the culture as they so desire. And it doesn't end after the service; the experience can last a lifetime. How a young (or old) American could spend two years in a foreign country very different from what is "normal" in the United States and *not* be changed is beyond me. I can still picture my village perfectly with its small cafes, the post office, the bus stop. I remember watching deep orange sunsets with my Basotho friends as we discussed local gossip, chasing tiny herdboys around in games of tag, and teaching students who used candles for illumination about the marvels of electric light bulbs.

Peace Corps volunteers always get asked "Why are you doing this?" Those who ask may never understand; the ones asked may never be able to explain it. I find it difficult to describe all the *good* reasons for being a volunteer because they are un-quantifiable. The reasons exist in the laughter of my students; the faces of gratitude from the villagers; the warmth and love I feel for my Basotho companions. I don't know if we are on the right road to solving developmental issues in Lesotho, but Peace Corps has garnered a lot of supporters over the past 22 years while the Basotho have earned a lot of friendships. To me it just feels good to be here. I know we could never mutually help and support each other by remaining home—so maybe it's simply a step in the right direction and a belief that we are all citizens of planet earth who can live together. I hope so.

Personal Growth and Development

> *Be patient toward all that is unsolved in your heart . . . try to love the questions themselves like locked rooms and like books that are written in a very foreign tongue. Do not now seek the answers, which cannot be given you because you would not be able to live them. And the point is, to live everything. Live the questions now. Perhaps you will then gradually, without noticing it, live along some distant day into the answer.*
>
> —*Rainer Marie Rilke*

A wonderful example of how volunteering can provide personal growth and development appeared in an article in the *Washington Post* entitled, "Taking Time to Give Time," by Neal Karlen. In it, Karlen told the story of Susan Gatten from San Francisco. When Gatten moved from South Bend, Indiana to San Francisco in 1970, she joined the Junior League. "I didn't join the San Francisco chapter out of some tremendous need to do something for the community. I just thought the League would give me a bunch of people to know in a new city." By day, Gatten worked as a corporate trainer for the Charles Schwab brokerage firm. By night, she began to do volunteer work such as working with Special Olympics, community projects in Chinatown, and with disadvantaged minority youngsters.

It was about this time that the AIDS epidemic hit San Francisco, and it did not personally affect her until a friend at Schwab's died of the disease in 1982. "I just had to do something. I'm not the Eleanor Roosevelt or Florence Nightingale type, but I couldn't just stand by and watch. I decided to do what I do best—organize and educate." (She has a master's degree in organizational communication.)

She started by getting the League to donate $35,000 to the Shanti Project, which provides health care support to those with AIDS. Then she nominated herself for president of the League and won. As president, she began educating the League members about the terrible devastation of the disease. (More San Franciscans have already died of AIDS than were killed in the great earthquake of 1906.) As a result, the League formed a speakers' bureau to reach the corporate community and trained members to counsel and care for people with AIDS. This was a growth experience for both groups.

Eventually, more than 100 San Francisco Junior League members became actively involved, and the League committed to donating more than $150,000 to AIDS over three years. But Gatten didn't stop there. In 1987, she proposed a resolution at the League's International Convention that the group's 170,000 members become involved in AIDS work—and the resolution passed.[3]

What a long and exciting journey of growth and learning she has taken—from 1970 when she joined the League for social reasons, to becoming an advocate for a cause in an international organization.

The opportunity to grow through volunteering crosses economic lines as well as cultural ones.

Winnie Brown, executive director of the New York City Mayor's Voluntary Action Center shared with me the following remarkable story about a homeless client of their clothing bank who, through volunteering, has become one of their key paid staff members.

Millie Mendez first approached the CLOTHING BANK: New Clothes for the Homeless, in New York City, when she was homeless herself and was looking for work. The apartment where she had lived had burned down and she was living in a public shelter for the homeless. She had also lost her job in a clothing factory. The center offered her a volunteer job sorting the thousands of new garments contributed by manufacturers for distribution to the needy. Millie's hard work as a volunteer impressed Winnie and other staff members so much they eventually offered her the first paid position with the clothing bank. She became a supervisor of the City Volunteer Corps team that unloads the clothing from the trucks, keeps inventory, and distributes to more than 350 shelters and nonprofit agencies.

In addition, Millie was so eager to get out of the shelter for homeless women and into a new single room occupancy residence (which had been built for people in her situation) that she volunteered to help out before the building even opened doing various odd jobs. Having only a third grade education, Millie also needed help with reading and writing. She was extremely eager to learn so Winnie enrolled her with Literacy Volunteers of New York City. She progressed so rapidly that she is now writing about her experiences and thoughts as a once-homeless person and had one of her pieces published in a book by Literacy Volunteers. She was also asked by Literacy Volunteers to help in the orientation of new students.

An excerpt from one of the pieces Millie wrote summarizes her feelings about learning and growing in even the most difficult situations—like homelessness:

> Now I feel so good about myself because I realize that it is never too late to be someone or to do something for yourself. Don't let your dreams die, go for it. Never give up. It is not easy and it will not happen in one day.

What these stories illustrate is that the process of learning and growing requires:

- An attitude of openness and optimism

- A willingness to seek out new experiences and not wait for them to come to you

- A readiness to risk

- An attitude of acceptance of different people and situations

- A belief that learning is meant to be life-long—and that we can, in fact, learn from everyone!

Creativity: A Pathway to Growth

One of the most enlightening movies I have seen is *Dead Poets' Society*. It is a provocative story about a staid New England boys' school and a maverick teacher, Mr. Keating (played beautifully by Robin Williams). Keating had a goal much larger than just teaching the boys English—he wanted them to grasp the excitement of learning and to discover the unique potential of each person. In one scene he had the boys go into the hall, where the pictures of all the past graduating classes were hung. He asked them all to lean in close to the pictures and listen very intently. "Make something extraordinary of your life," he whispered loudly, *"Carpe diem!"* (seize the day). It was a powerful scene.

At one point in the movie, the headmaster confronted Keating and asked him what he thought he was accomplishing through all his "antics" (like having the boys stand on their desks to get a different view of the world). He asked Keating what he believed education was really about. "To help these boys learn to think for themselves," Keating replied. The headmaster sternly admonished him, saying that education is to teach discipline, to pass on tradition, and prepare the boys to get into college.

The movie poignantly depicted the struggle between

growth and stagnation in individuals and institutions.

One of the real dangers of not being open to the risk of learning and trying out new things is that we might die before we have really lived! Eric Fromm once said, "Most people die before they are fully born. Creativeness means to be born before one dies . . . without courage and faith— creativity is impossible."

When it comes to this business of creativity, we need to learn from our children. Researchers tell us that the most creative people in the world are kids under five. Abraham Maslow once observed:

> Give an adult a hammer and we treat the whole world like a nail. Give a child a hammer and they may dig with it, sculpt with it, weigh down papers with leaves in between or knock down apples with it, because nobody told them it was to hit a nail.

What are the traits that make young children so creative?

- **Curiosity**
- **High energy**
- **Enthusiasm**
- **Imagination**
- **Almost no fear of failure**
- **High level of risk-taking**
- **Humor**
- **Persistence**

Their favorite word in the English language is "why" and they ask it relentlessly. Unfortunately, as the movie I mentioned depicted, the traditional school system too often curbs this creativity. "Children enter school as question marks and leave as periods," says educator Neil Postman. How very sad. It is important that we turn ourselves back into question marks and realize the value and necessity of creativity and life-long learning.

The one absolute necessity for creative thinking at any age is imagination. How can we hope to change the world, or even a small corner of it, unless we can clearly and vividly imagine the way we'd like it to be? "Imagination is more important than knowledge," Einstein said, "for knowledge is limited to all we know and understand, while imagination embraces the entire world—and all there ever will be to know and understand."

I cannot talk about the creativity and imagination of youngsters without sharing a couple of stories about our kids when they were under age five.

I stated earlier that *persistence* was one of the traits of creativity. When our daughter Lisa was a toddler, I was determined to teach her to leave vases, ashtrays, and other fragile items alone so that we could take her to other homes without living in fear of disaster. She kept picking up anything within reach with great determination, so I began gently spanking her hand when she did it. She soon figured out how to manage that—she'd reach for something, stop a moment, slap her own hand, and then continue on with her mission. Persistence was her middle name!

Richard, our son, had an imaginary friend named George, who was very real to him between the ages of three and five. George sat at the table with us, went on trips with us, and did just about everything else with us. One day I watched while Richard took his imaginary friend on a tour of an elaborate toy village he had built. Stopping at one building, he explained to George, "And this is the Standard Gas Station that Jesus visited in 1932." (Where does something like that come from? A wonderful, vivid imagination.) By the way, George's leave-taking was just as creative. One day, when we were all in the car ready to start on a trip, Richard announced from the back seat that George was not with us because he had gone to Alaska and got married. And that was the end of George.

I've shared these stories to help you recall your favorite stories about your own children or other children you have known. Recapture the memories so you can learn from them. Better still, teach a class of four- or five-year-olds, volunteer in a day-care center, or become a Big Brother or Big Sister to a lonely child. They have so much to teach us.

I remember reading this quote when my children were little: "I brought this three-year-old into the world—I might as well let her show it to me."

Roles of Creative Thinking & Learning

In one of his popular books on creativity, *A Kick in the Seat of the Pants*, Roger von Oech outlines four roles we as adults need to be able to play if we are to think more creatively:[4]

- **The Explorer**
- **The Artist**
- **The Judge**
- **The Warrior**

The Explorer—In this role, you search for new information, data, ideas and as many new experiences as possible. (Volunteering can be one of those valuable new experiences.)

My late husband Harvey and I felt it necessary to keep stretching and growing, both personally and as a couple, so we used our holidays to try out new experiences. For example, the last several years of our 33 years together, we snorkeled at the Great Barrier Reef in Australia, were passengers on an eight-day whitewater river raft trip through the Grand Canyon, and parasailed in Greece.

Each of those activities made me overcome some fear, stretch my horizons, and flex my aging mental and physical muscles. And each time, I came back with renewed energy, increased confidence in my abilities, and a broader perspective. They were experiences that promoted both learning and growth, and they were a great deal of fun! (How thankful I am now that we did not wait until retirement to have these adventures.)

Now I'll ask you. What new things have you tried lately? If your answer is, "not much," try out something new, whether it be for fun or for a challenge. Volunteering for an organization is one option and it might be the "kick in the seat of the pants" you've needed!

The Artist—When you are in this role, you are learning to adapt and apply the new information and experiences to your own life situation, using your own uniqueness, knowledge, skill, and flare. In other words, you use what you learned as an explorer to help you do what you do more creatively. This is when you let that five-year-old in you loose. As an explorer, I went parasailing, seeing when I was high in the air that Greece was right next to Albania. (I couldn't see that from the ground.) As an artist, I've learned to recapture that experience when I've got a problem and can't seem to find the solution because I'm too close to it. I try to mentally parasail, and get above the situation so that I can see the whole picture. It changes my perspective and often triggers a new insight. Someone once said, "It's difficult to see the picture when you stay inside the frame."

The Judge—It's important not to get into this role too soon. At this stage you objectively evaluate the merits of the new ideas you created as artist. This is when you prune, change, add, or delete to make the idea an even better, more workable concept. Many people do this too quickly and thus shut down the creative process. Be flamboyant in your ideas. Dream first—get practical later.

The Warrior—It is the warrior in you that carries your new idea into action. This is where the faint-hearted fall by the wayside, since introducing something new means something old must die. That usually means we have to fight for what we believe. And there are always the three S's waiting in the wings, ready to kill the idea: the system, the status quo, and the stinkers. (It's been said, "When you go to make your mark on the world, beware of people with erasers!") As my friend Doris Pierson said, "We as volunteers too often underestimate the significant influence we can have as 'warriors' in bringing about needed change. We do not have a job on the line, we can go anywhere to influence on behalf of our cause, and we are voters—a powerful combination!" Doris knows, since she has been a life-long volunteer herself—serving on school boards, in city government, in school substance abuse programs, and in her church.

These are important concepts for those of us concerned about the myriad of problems facing our communities today. What we need are new, innovative solutions. And volunteers are often the people who have the fresh insights and ideas to spark new solutions.

Youth Learn & Grow Through Giving

Learning through the joy of giving is not restricted to adults. More and more communities are discovering that one of the most powerful antidotes to the alienation of our youth is to offer them meaningful and worthwhile learning opportunities through community service as early as possible. Many of the problems besieging young people today (alcohol and other drugs, suicide, teen pregnancy, violence) are related to self-esteem. Not knowing who they are or how they fit into today's complex society, it is easy for them to escape into the numbing non-reality of drugs, rebellion, or apathy. Unfortunately, these are often the only youth we hear about and read about.

One of the best kept secrets in America is that there is another enormous group of young people who are actively involved in being part of the solution instead of the problem. According to a report issued by the Commission on Youth and America's Future, the numbers are impressive, and are growing steadily:

- High school students contribute 17 million hours of unpaid volunteer service annually.

- College students donate 192 million hours annually.

- Members in Youth Corps, who work in national parks, conservation, etc., perform 41 million hours of community service yearly.

The report goes on to say, "When young people have a chance to act on their humanitarian ideals, they build self-respect and strong attachments to family and community. There is virtually no limit to what young people with appropriate education, training, and encouragement—can do, no social need they cannot help meet. We reiterate: Young people are essential resources, and society needs their active participation as citizens."[5]

It is also true that just as society needs the contributions of our youth, young people need the experience of volunteering. This is beautifully illustrated by the comments of a Minneapolis eighth-grader involved in an innovative program of community service called Teen Outreach:

> In Teen Outreach you learn how to give time to help others. I never thought I could be of much help to anybody because I sometimes feel like I have too many problems myself. But helping others helps me too. It feels good and it shows I can do okay at things, even though I don't always do okay with school work.[6]

This issue of youth involvement has become a national priority. There have been numerous bills before Congress relating to some form of youth community service. I will discuss this further in chapter 9.

Schools Promote Volunteerism

More and more schools and colleges are acknowledging volunteering as a valuable learning experience. This new and encouraging attitude is reflected in the following examples:

—David Warren, president of Ohio Wesleyan University, stated in a 1989 letter to students:

> Perhaps the most gratifying development on our campus this year has been the participation of more than 1,000 of our 1,800 students in volunteer work. Our students are increasingly interested in community service and the exercise of citizenship . . . I believe that some kind of community service is integral to the liberal arts, both as a means of putting theory into practice and also, simply as a way of contributing to the community we all share. Public service is a strength, and a value, that our students will carry with them long after they leave Ohio Wesleyan.

—Auburn University in Montgomery, Alabama, has a service-learning course entitled, "Social Work with the Homeless" which links classroom study with volunteer work. The goal of the program is to give students an opportunity to apply their academic knowledge to the very real and difficult problems associated with the homeless in Montgomery. Students help the Salvation Army by interviewing people, filling out forms, issuing clothing vouchers, registering people for the soup kitchen, and checking people into the shelter at night. They also arrange transportation, locate jobs and housing, and make referrals to social service agencies. The students have the opportunity to discuss these experiences in weekly seminars and are required to write a paper on the homeless situation. "I know I can't save the world," one student said, "but if I can take the wrinkles off one person's brow, then I have done something."[7]

—The University of Pennsylvania Law School requires all students to perform 70 hours of unpaid professional service before they can graduate. The program is expected to provide 15,000 hours of free legal service each year to nonprofit organizations, the homeless, etc. "We see the program as a way to show students they can get ahead and do well and still donate time to public service," said Howard Lesnick, chairman of the school's educational committee. Several law school deans commented that their students are beginning to show more public-mindedness than they've seen in ten years. Some of the other law schools that have active volunteer involvement are Tulane University Law School, University of California Law School, and Northwestern University School of Law.[8]

—Campus Outreach Opportunity League (COOL) was founded in 1982 to help college students become involved in their local communities. Founder of COOL, Wayne Meisel, who was a volunteer while at Harvard, felt that by working on local needs such as homelessness, hunger, health, environment, literacy, and education, students could learn how to make a significant difference in the lives of others. He personally hiked from Maine to Washington D.C., visiting 65 colleges along the way, to generate interest in student volunteering. Now with a small paid staff of recent college graduates, COOL develops and provides technical assistance (such as a booklet called "Building a Movement: Students in Community Service," and a quarterly newsletter called "Campus Outreach"), and conducts workshops for colleges and universities around the country on student volunteering and leadership development. This outstanding program was a 1987 President's Volunteer Action Award winner. To contact COOL, write: COOL, 386 McNeal Hall, University of Minnesota, St. Paul, Minnesota 55708, or call (612) 624-3018.

—Holy Cross High School in Flushing, New York, has a course called Community Service Preparation, which has become a tradition. The vast majority of seniors not only take the course, which is required, but also spend 75 hours volunteering in the community for extra academic credit. "The sensitivity they gain is necessary for each boy's own growth and personal development," their instructor commented. Since students work primarily with the sick, handicapped, and elderly, they are carefully trained for their work through activities like maneuvering wheelchairs; trying to speak with marshmallows in their mouths to understand speech impediments; and listening to quick, garbled instructions to learn how things might sound to the mentally retarded. One student, Mark Angelini, worked in an educational/recreational program for the blind, and commented:

> We were expecting a bunch of old blind people yelling. They gave their picture of the world to us, telling us about opera and word games, blowing our minds with what they knew. They were teaching us instead of us teaching them.

"For kids who in a way have everything," Michael Genovese, director of the program, observed, "community work gives them a piece of the world they don't have." Student Fabian Reyes added, "It's funny to see the big change in attitudes here between freshman and senior year. You come in being waited on, you come out serving."[9]

Learning and growing can and should be a life-long journey. In order to make these a part of your life it is necessary to maintain a positive attitude, seek out new experiences, be willing to risk, and think creatively.

Autobiography in Five Short Chapters

I. I walk down the street.
There is a deep hole in the sidewalk.
I fall in.
I am lost . . . I am helpless.
It isn't my fault.
It takes forever to find a way out.

II. I walk down the same street.
There is a deep hole in the sidewalk.
I pretend I don't see it.
I fall in, again.
I can't believe I am in this same place.
But it isn't my fault.
It still takes a long time to get out.

III. I walk down the same street.
There is a deep hole in the sidewalk.
I see it is there.
I still fall in . . . it's a habit . . . but,
my eyes are open.
I know where I am.
It is my fault.
I get out immediately.

IV. I walk down the same street.
There is a deep hole in the sidewalk.
I walk around it.

V. I walk down another street.

—Author Unknown

—•5•—

Putting Your Beliefs
Into Action

*The actual transformation of our convictions and
beliefs into action is a difficult path. The thing that
lies at the foundation of positive change, the way I
see it, is service to a fellow human being.*

—Lech Walesa

Can you name the key turning points in your life—those
forks in the road where your decision to take a specific
path changed your life?

Throughout my lifetime, I have found that these
decisions have often been directly related to having to put
my own personal beliefs into action—of having to *do* what I
say I *believe*. This chapter is initially about my personal
experiences, because I believe I can best make my point by
sharing my own personal story. I am a Christian, however,
I hope you will be able to relate to these experiences based
on your own personal belief system, whatever your spiritual
or religious background.

Putting My Own Beliefs Into Action

One of the most significant turning points for me began in a very ordinary, almost mundane way. I was reading my church magazine, *The Lutheran Standard*, when I stumbled onto an article that changed the direction of my life forever.

This particular article was entitled "You're Asking Me What Poverty Is!" It was written by a woman who had lived in poverty all her life. She graphically described what it felt like, smelled like, and tasted like—and then she shared her despair at seeing her children being caught in the same cycle of poverty and not knowing how to help them break out of it. She ended by saying, "I did not come from another time. I did not come from another place. I am here, now, and there are others like me all around you."[1]

As I laid the magazine down, I realized with a sense of shock that I did not personally know any of these people. They were not in my beautiful mountain neighborhood, nor were they in our affluent, university-area church. Where were they? Who were they? And even more importantly, what was *I* to do about it?

I found that I could not utter my usual perfunctory prayer: "Lord, please help the poor people." Instead, I said perhaps the most important prayer of my life: "Lord, I am available!" This time there was no bargaining and no preconceived ideas about what I could or should do. I simply knew that this had my name on it and my beliefs were on the line. It was time to "walk the talk" about what I said I believed.

I realize now that I had finally learned to pray the prayer of hope and trust. In his excellent book on prayer, *With Open Hands*, Henri Nouwen says:

> When we live with hope we do not get tangled up with concerns for how our wishes will be fulfilled . . . Hope includes an openness where you wait for the promise to be delivered, even though you never know when, where, or how this might happen.[2]

I had to totally trust God, as I know Him, to lead me as I tried to discover which people in our community were in need, what it was they were in need of, and what I had to offer that might be helpful. This journey of faith brought me, in just two short months, to a group of people who were struggling to start the Boulder County Volunteer and Information Center. Most of them were human service professionals who were well-acquainted with the unmet needs of their clients. The one thing they lacked was the time necessary to organize and launch the center. Time was something I had in abundance, since both our children were in school and I was not employed at the time. I was also new to Boulder and eager to get involved. Along with my time and enthusiasm, I also brought six years of organizational skills developed working in human resource management before our children were born.

So, along with two other people, I agreed to volunteer thirty hours a week for three months to get the center organized. A large group of other volunteers joined us, and the center became a reality. When we were ready to open, the group asked me to become the first executive director, and I happily accepted. During my seven years at the center, my questions—Who are these poor people? What do they really need? What can I do to help?—were answered. We not only found volunteers to help at most of the volunteer agencies and nonprofit organizations in the community, but also worked directly with clients to help them find the services they needed. Where no service existed, we recruited volunteers, churches, or service clubs to fill the need. We also helped fill unusual requests, like volunteer electrical and plumbing repairs, and emergency transportation. If something was needed, we found it. Need and poverty were no longer theoretical concepts to me, but a day-to-day, person-to-person reality.

It was this experience that deepened my commitment to volunteerism, both in the community and in my church, and led me to write three books and conduct more than 1,000 training events on the subject of volunteer management. This stepping out in faith not only led me to use the skills I already had, but helped me discover and develop abilities I never dreamed I possessed. I thank God for that magazine article—and my simple prayer.

When it comes to identifying our own gifts and abilities and giving them to a Higher Power to use, it is natural that we resist. First, it sounds bold and boastful to say we're good at something. Secondly, we may honestly feel we have no gifts or talents at all and believe there is nothing much we could do. And perhaps most importantly, it is scary to "let go" of ourselves and become open to being "led."

One of my favorite stories is about a young high school student who was teaching Sunday School at his church for the first time. He was nervously poring over the lesson on Saturday evening, and his mother asked him what he was going to teach his third-graders the next day. "Well," he said, "the book says to tell them that each of us has certain skills, talents, and abilities that God can use, and that everyone of us is unique and special." Then he paused and added, "And if that doesn't work, I guess we'll make clay bunnies!"

My guess is, many people would rather make clay bunnies, or clean the house, or mow the lawn, or clean out a garage, or go skiing, or even become a workaholic, than deal with the difficult task of discovering what their unique abilities and talents are and how they might use them in helping others.

In her book *Eighth Day of Creation*, Elizabeth O'Connor summarizes this dilemma beautifully:

> Commitment at the point of my gifts means that I must give up being a straddler. Somewhere in the deeps of me I know this. Life will not be the smorgasbord I have made it, sampling and tasting here and there. My commitment will give me an identity.[3]

Do What You Can With What You Have

As a teenager, I remember worrying about what I should do with my life. When I would hear a sermon about "turning your life over to God," I would immediately envision the consequences. I'd probably end up in Africa as a missionary or something equally exotic. That was too frightening to contemplate. I loved my life in Montana and being with my family and friends. Africa had no appeal at all! It was not until years later that I realized the truth shared by Paul Scherer:

> You aren't likely to be sent out under the will of God to do startling, impossible things. You are likely to be sent out to do the quiet, unspectacular things that matter, precisely where you are and with what you have![4]

And Mother Teresa of Calcutta would seem to agree:

> To show great love for God and neighbors we need not do great things. It is how much love we put in the doing that makes our offering something beautiful for God.[5]

One of the best-known and most widely-respected men of recent times is Lech Walesa. He is an excellent example of someone who did not set out with a mission to do something spectacular, but because he was willing to put his beliefs into action, ended up leading a nation and changing history.

This previously unknown and ordinary Polish electrician worked in the shipyards of Gdansk. He founded the Solidarity labor union and spent almost a year in detention in the process. A devout Roman Catholic who takes daily communion, Walesa believes simply that he has the God-given mission of leadership to fulfill for the Polish people he loves. He was willing to share what he had and who he was to help fight for the freedom of the Polish people. In 1981, he was chosen as *Time* magazine's "Man of the Year," and he later received the Nobel Peace Prize.

I'd like to share some of his comments about his beliefs contained in a story about him in *The Courage of Conviction*, by Phillip Berman:

Faith is the sole meaning of my life . . . if I did not believe in the Creator and in all that we profess in our Christian credo, then all that I am would be meaningless and pointless. I would be nothing. All that I do I do because I have faith. That does not mean I am a saint; just as every human, I make mistakes, many mistakes.

. . . On my path, I have encountered some wonderful, brave, great people who astounded me with their deductive powers. I have also met people less gifted, yet each and every one of them is necessary in their own position. It is not just me who needs these people. It is our cause as a whole, all our nation, who needs these people, their gifts and talents.[6]

In this story, Walesa also illustrates the beautiful metamorphosis than can occur when one dares to step out on belief, even though he or she does not feel qualified for the challenge.

Prior to the formation of Solidarity, Walesa says he was incapable of saying anything in public. "Come August, things changed. I don't know how it happened!" says this man who has become an international spokesman for freedom. On November 15, 1989, he became the second private citizen ever to be allowed to address the U.S. Congress, and received four standing ovations during his stirring speech. He is an inspiration to many of us, and is an excellent example of an ordinary person putting his beliefs into action and making an *extraordinary* difference.

Thoughts About Beliefs In Action

The theme of putting beliefs into action seems to exist throughout much of the spiritual thinking world:

> *For the seeker of truth, there are certain beliefs that must accompany every action: one should act without selfishness, cultivate compassion for all living things and develop respect for others. I believe all religions carry the same message despite their differences in philosophy . . . Our beliefs as well as our actions must come from the heart, for in our hearts the true wisdom that frees us and the path of compassion are inseparable.*
>
> *—The 14th Dalai Lama of Tibet*

> *Live your beliefs and you can turn the world around.*
>
> *—Henry Thoreau*

> *Faith in action is love and love in action is service and proof of service is peace.*
>
> *—Mother Theresa*

> *There's a difference between interest and commitment. When you're interested in doing something, you do it only when it's convenient. When you're committed to something, you accept no excuses, only results.*
>
> *—Kenneth Blanchard, author*

As I view it, life is not divided into neat, separate categories of belief and action. The test of belief is action and the motivation of action is belief. Indeed, the whole of cognitive living is belief in action. Belief unaccompanied by action is sterile. Action that is not rooted in belief is like a building without a firm foundation, in danger of collapsing under the strains and stresses of life experience.

—Israel Goldstein
(one of the founders of the National Conference of Christians and Jews)

Integrate what you believe in every single area of your life. Take your heart to work and ask the most and best of everybody else too. Don't let your special character and values, the secret that you know and no one else does, the truth—don't let that get swallowed up by the great chewing complacency.

—Meryl Streep, actress

The great end of life is not knowledge but action.

—Thomas Huxley

The proof of God is in the rejection of nothingness. We are not children of relativity. We are children of God. And we are brothers. And we enjoy or suffer the consequences of our ideas, our acts, our hopes, and our fears . . . I cannot affirm God if I fail to affirm man . . . The sense of human unity makes possible a reverence for life.

—Norman Cousins

Steve Allen, often called "TV's Renaissance Man" because he is a composer, author, humanitarian, actor, comedian, and philosopher, wrote this about the inexhaustible nature of love and what happens when one puts love into action:

> God is love, you said. Or God is electricity. I do not know what God is. All I hope is that He knows what I am. Electric force can be both measured and diminished. Love cannot, at least not in that way.
>
> When the first child was born, I loved it. But when the second child was born I found I loved not half as much but just as much.
>
> And when the third arrived, he, too, received full share. So love's a magic force that knows no laws, a well without a bottom, a purse that's never empty. Use your own cliché. Just so you get the point.
>
> And one point more remains to make: that like the other faculties, the physical, the musical, the social, and the rest, love swells in action. Will sets it aflame;
>
> It grows in height, direction, depth, and kind. It is the wise and wholly just investment.[7]

Sharing Your Gifts With Others

In the Old Testament, God's message to the patriarch Abraham was, "You are blessed to be a blessing." For me, this statement sums up the rightful relationship between receiving and giving—between beliefs and action. I believe that each of us has been given unique abilities, talents, and opportunities. The true joy of these gifts is only realized when we share them with others. Hoarding or ignoring them brings nothing to anyone, including ourselves. We simply become miserly and distrustful—fearful of others who want or need what we have. This is illustrated well by Earl Loomis in his book *The Self in Pilgrimage*:

> Goodness makes claims. It must be expressed. It must be used . . . the man who knows he could help others but helps only himself will ultimately not be able to live with himself . . . What we do not use is wasted; what we do not share we cannot keep.[8]

If it is true that faith needs to be in action and that love must find a way to serve, what are some options for the ordinary person who wants to serve others? In his book *Celebration of Discipline*, Richard Foster lists the following possibilities. He cautions, however, that "Service that is duty-motivated breathes death. Service that flows out of our inward person is life, joy and peace."[9]

SIMPLE WAYS TO SERVE OTHERS

1. The service of hiddenness

These are the acts of service or gifts of money that are shared anonymously—for the joy of giving. It doesn't matter who gets the credit. Foster says, "If all of our serving is before others we will be shallow people indeed."

2. The service of small things

These are the seemingly insignificant day-to-day opportunities to help that surround each of us in our homes, communities, places of work, and religious organizations. It is "pitching in" and "lending a hand"—and though it may not seem important, these create the climate we live in daily. The extent to which we do this creates either a climate that feels good (because we care enough about one another to help however we can), or one that makes us feel cold, lonely, and competitive.

3. The service of guarding the reputation of others

This is the commitment to keep from the back-biting and gossip that can so easily destroy individuals and groups. Have you ever noticed the terrible tendency people have to try to destroy leaders? I am not talking about the horrifying assassinations of national leaders many of us have witnessed in our lifetimes—but the all too common tendency to slowly "kill off" people with words and innuendos and accusations. The old playground chant, "Sticks and stones may break my bones, but words will never hurt me," is simply untrue. Words can kill people. They can destroy a person's confidence, self-esteem, initiative, hope, and eventually, even their health. Let's serve one another by sharing our concerns and dissatisfactions directly with the person involved. This means talking *to* them, not *about* them.

4. The service of being served

We have had the notion that it is more noble to give than to receive drummed into us so often that we have forgotten it can also be a blessing to be the receiver. One can't be blessed through giving if no one will receive. And if we feel that we must always be the one giving help, it may say something about our pride. This was a lesson I learned anew as I gratefully accepted the love and kindness of friends in the aftermath of my husband Harvey's death. Through that experience, I developed a deeper understanding of what is really helpful, and learned the subtle difference between "caring for" and "taking care of" another person. In the end, I realized that my helpers had become my teachers.

5. The service of common courtesy—(or should we say uncommon courtesy?)

How precious courtesy has become in our hurried world. When a clerk smiles, when a waitress brings a second cup of coffee, when a driver lets you into the stream of traffic, when a flight attendant holds a cranky baby for a tired mother— how much nicer the day becomes for all of us. "Please," "thank you," "excuse me"—whatever words or actions will affirm someone else's worth—are gifts of service.

6. The service of hospitality

We need to do more than just take turns having one another over for coffee or a meal. To be hospitable means opening our homes and our lives to others. It is the business of having homes (versus houses) which are places of refuge and renewal for all who enter there—and inviting as many as possible to share it with you. Harvey and I changed our attitudes toward entertaining the last few years of our marriage. We did almost no "duty entertaining" (i.e. we ought to have them over for business or social reasons). Our hosting became casual and comfortable with emphasis and time invested in the guests, conversation, and being together instead of in having a spotless house, an elegant dinner, and faultless serving.

7. The service of listening

One of the greatest gifts we can give to another person is allowing them to tell us about themselves. We live in a society of strangers, where small talk abounds. How the world needs listeners—those who have the gift of non-possessive caring. This is something every one of us can do, every single day. Henri Nouwen describes this way of serving beautifully:

> . . . when we honestly ask ourselves which persons in our lives mean the most to us, we often find that it is those who, instead of giving much advice, solutions, or

cures, have chosen rather to share our pain and touch our wounds with a gentle and tender hand. The friend who can be silent with us in a moment of despair or confusion, who can stay with us in an hour of grief and bereavement, who can tolerate not-knowing, not-curing, not-healing, and face us with the reality of our powerlessness, that is the friend who cares.

8. The service of sharing the word of life with one another

I recently heard a theologian say that today's Christians are too often like fishermen who camp next to a big lake full of fish, build a fish house, and spend all their time debating how to fish . . . but they never get at fishing!

Too often we feel we must play several frightening roles in order to share our beliefs with one another. We must be:

• An *attorney* who can argue the case

• A *jury* to decide guilt or innocence

• A *judge* who determines points of law

When in reality, all we are to be is a *witness*, sharing what we have experienced in *our* lives. To be effective, we need to simply and honestly try to tell our own stories, whatever they may be.

9. The service of bearing the burdens of each other

This is illustrated throughout this entire book—in the numerous examples of people in all walks of life who have taken the time and energy to reach out to someone else in need—sharing and even easing their burdens. In his book, *The Wounded Healer*, Henri Nouwen says that to help one another in our contemporary society:

> We must be able to avoid the distance of pity as well
> as the exclusiveness of sympathy. Compassion is born
> when we discover in the center of our own existence not
> only that God is God and man is man, but also that our
> neighbor really is our fellow man.[10]

These have been examples of simple ways in which to serve or help others. What are some other ways in which you can serve others as a volunteer? This book is full of examples of needs. Chapter 1 alone lists well over 100 opportunities and suggestions for volunteer service in agencies and organizations in every community. Most of the people whose stories I've shared throughout this book are volunteering because of a compelling love for others and a belief in some power greater than themselves. The opportunities are endless, if you are ready to see them and reach out to others.

Helping in Religious Organizations

Another way to put your beliefs into action is to volunteer within your own religious organization. Many such organizations are changing the way they look at the involvement of their members. They are finally looking at their members as volunteers, and are eager to learn more about working effectively with them.

Since publishing my last book, *How to Mobilize Church Volunteers*, I have been deluged with requests from religious groups across this country and Canada to provide workshops on the topics that I normally do for secular volunteer programs. These include sessions on all aspects of effective management and motivation of volunteers. In both the secular and religious worlds, it is obvious that good intentions are no longer enough. Organizations of all types must use people's limited time efficiently.

For those of you who are or would like to be involved in volunteering *within* your church, synagogue, or religious organization, the options today are becoming more exciting and varied. The opportunities listed below have been taken from recruiting bulletins and brochures from groups in my training sessions:

VOLUNTEER OPTIONS

Board or committee member
Teacher: religious school, Sunday school
Sunday morning assistant with children
Choir member
Church librarian
Greeter
Hospitality room host or hostess
Organist
Liturgist
Volunteer coordinator
Computer programmer
Usher
Parent advisory council member
Sunday school class sponsor/university ministry
Youth counselor/sponsor
Adopt-a-college student sponsor
Adult working with youth in special ministries
Advent workshop organizer
"Bigger Kids" recreation program coordinator
Care Canteen—older adult ministry volunteer
Ritual/worship volunteer
Social action committee member
Hebrew teacher
Women's/men's fellowship group member
Brotherhood/sisterhood organizations volunteer
Song leader
Child development program assistant
Church archives volunteer
Church blood club supporter
Coach or athletic instructor
Communications and advocacy volunteer

Food services volunteer
Home visitation volunteer
Hospital visitation volunteer
Interviewer
Arts programmer
Respite care giver
Supply room coordinator/visual arts librarian
Transportation ministry volunteer
Visual arts volunteer
Vacation Bible school teachers
Summer reading program coordinator
Field trip coordinator
Day camp counselor
Children's music & arts volunteer
Youth drama group coordinator
Junior counselor for day camp
Coordinator of service projects for youth
Photographer
Newsletter editor/writer
Bible study leader
Altar guild member
Guitarist
Sports team member
Youth choir member
Handbell choir member
Clothing drive organizer
Coffee hour organizer
Care giver for the homeless and hungry
Jobs network coordinator
Lay pastoral care program volunteer
Mission education programs volunteer
Monday night caller
Office volunteer
Peace task force member
Mitzvah corps member
Teen Teletrouble telephone counselor
Thrift shop clerk

If you want to become more involved in your spiritual community, don't be shy or overly humble. If your religious organization has a volunteer coordinator (and more and more are getting them), start there for an overview of needs and options. This person can serve as a guide to match you with an appropriate volunteer opportunity. If you don't have one, share your interest in becoming involved with the minister, rabbi, priest, or others involved in leadership. If you are interested in a leadership position, let them know.

The Problem of Pillars and Pew-sitters

Unfortunately, sometimes when people reach out to become involved, they fall through the cracks. When that happens, we all lose. This true story illustrates what I mean:

> I moved here about a year and a half ago to live with my daughter and her family. This was after my husband passed away. One of the first things I did was join a church here. I'm a member of a different denomination than my daughter, but I found a church of my own close to our home. When I first joined, they asked me to fill out a form listing my interests and talents and how I'd be willing to serve this new church. I put down quite a long list because I'd been very active in my old congregation and I now had lots of time on my hands. I was also eager to feel like I belonged in my new church family. It's been one and a half years and nobody has ever called to ask me to do anything. It's really very sad!

These were the words of a lovely silver-haired lady in one of my audiences where the topic was "Volunteerism in the Church." It made me want to weep—it was such a waste of a person's gifts and willingness to share! As the workshop participants discussed her comments, it became clear to us why organizations of all types frequently have difficulty getting more than a handful of people involved. Often there is a group of "doers" who simply—wittingly or not—continue to ask each other instead of seeking out others who might be willing to help when a need arises. (In a recent survey, it was found that 70 percent of people who claim church membership in this country are in no way involved in their congregation except for occasional attendance at services.) I call this the phenomenon of "the pillars and the pew sitters," and it has become a major problem in many religious organizations today.

Most theologies strongly endorse the belief that each human being is unique and has gifts and talents that are needed and should be shared. However, too many organizations are still operating with only a handful of members doing everything. This must change if they are to be alive and well in the new century. Let's help that happen!

Whether you want to become involved as a volunteer within a religious setting or in your community, there are opportunities for anyone who wants to put their own beliefs into action. However you choose to go about finding the "need with your name on it," it is important that you do it with a sense of love and commitment, and with *passion.* Perhaps we can learn best, once again, from a child:

Five years old, sitting at the kitchen table, elbows table-edge, chin in hands, tears glistening in those dark eyes.

"You want to tell me about it?" I ventured.
Small Voice: "I got my feelings hurt."
"Did somebody say something to you?"
Louder now: "Yes . . . the teacher said that some children have big tummies swollen sick because they don't have enough to eat."

Tears rolling down the face now: "When I grow up I'm going to give all my money to the children who

don't have enough to eat, because when they don't
have enough to eat, I get my feelings hurt."

O God in Heaven, hear your child. Five years old . . .
How did he know what some of us never learn?

That it's only when our feelings are hurt that we will
do something. When our feelings are hurt . . . when
we feel the hurt . . . we are willing to do something like
live out our faith in the hope of a day when all the
children of the earth will be fed.

I hope you get your feelings hurt . . .[11]

—Ann Weems

—•6•—

Helping a Cause
You Care About

*You can't plough a field by turning it over
in your mind.*

—Anonymous

One of the most remarkable stories I have encountered
was an article about a little girl in Philadelphia that I
read in *Guideposts* magazine more than 25 years ago:

> In a tenement district some years ago a clergyman
> started a Sunday school for neighborhood children. A
> little girl came to the very first meeting, but the meeting
> room was small and a number of other children had to
> be turned away. Hattie May Wiatt went to bed that night
> unhappy because her less fortunate playmates had no
> place to go to hear about Jesus.
>
> Always rather weak, Hattie May died two years later,
> and her parents sent for the minister. They handed him
> a worn, red pocketbook they had found beneath her

pillow. In it were exactly 57 pennies and a note scrawled in Hattie May's childish hand: "This is to help build the little church bigger so more children can go to Sunday School." For two years this frail child had run errands to help her neighbors. The pennies she had earned had all been carefully saved.

The next Sunday the minister carried the cracked, red pocketbook into his pulpit. He took out the 57 pennies and dropped them one by one back into the purse. Then he told about the little girl who gave all she had. The congregation was deeply touched.

After the service a guest came forward and offered some very desirable land for a new church building, saying, "I will let the church have it for a fraction of its value. The down payment is exactly fifty-seven pennies."

When the story was told in the newspapers, checks came in from far and wide. Now visitors to Philadelphia are impressed by the Temple Baptist Church with a seating capacity of 3,300, by Temple University with hundreds of students, by the Good Samaritan Hospital, by a Sunday School building large enough to accommodate every child who wants to attend. And it all began with a little girl who wanted to help others and found an answer to the question, What can I do?

This story was part of an article written by Dr. Norman Vincent Peale entitled, "What One Person Can Do." He noted how many people are overwhelmed and discouraged when looking at the enormity of problems like poverty, crime, pollution, and drugs. Too many feel that the efforts of one person really don't count. Dr. Peale stated:

One person can make a difference. One person can move mountains. I've seen it again and again. All you need to do is recognize a need, roll up your sleeves, ask God to help you, then plunge in with optimism and determination and enthusiasm. You don't have to be a big shot. You don't have to have a lot of influence. You just have to have faith in your power to change things. If that faith is strong enough, you *will* change things.[1]

Many people find tremendous satisfaction volunteering for a cause they care about. But sometimes people have a difficult time determining which cause they want to help. By asking yourself a few questions, you may find the cause that is right for you.

What do you care about deeply enough to want to change? Another way of asking that is—what is your passion? What stirs your heart, mind, and soul so deeply that you find yourself asking, What can *I* do about this need or problem? How can *I* help? This is different from the common intellectual response, Why don't *they* (the government, legal system, church, etc.) do something about it?

Dealing with this important question will help you narrow the field of possible involvement, so that whether you have a great deal of time or money to invest in a cause, or just a small amount, you will direct it to something that matters to *you*. This is sometimes referred to as "the need with your name on it," and has so much to do with the amount of satisfaction you will feel as a result of your involvement.

Many of you will recall the remarkable story of Trevor Ferrell. At just 11 years of age, he was so moved watching a television report on the homeless in Philadelphia that he started going out on the streets of his city night after night with blankets, pillows, and food that he was able to gather from friends and neighbors. His story was picked up by the media and became such an inspiration that someone donated a 33-room boarding house for the homeless that is now known as "Trevor's Place," and thousands of dollars in donations have poured in for the project. Trevor is an incredible example of someone who saw a need, was deeply moved, and *did something about it!*

Where are People Volunteering Today?

As I noted earlier, the causes and needs today are almost endless, and people make very individual choices about where to direct their time and energy. In the Gallup Survey on volunteering, the following information was tabulated on where volunteers invested their time in 1987. Obviously, there is something for everyone:[2]

Distribution of Volunteers and Assignments
By Activity Area in 1987

Religious Organizations	16%
Informal (neighborhood, self-help)	15%
Health	13%
Education	12%
Social Services/Welfare	10%
Recreation	8%
Civic, Social, Fraternal Organizations	7%
Political	4%
Arts, Culture, Humanities	4%
Work-Related Organizations	4%
Community Action	3%
Miscellaneous Fund Raising	3%
Foundations	1%
International, Foreign	1%

How to Choose Your Cause

Once you have chosen the category of need that is most important to you, there are other decisions to make:

1. **What particular aspect of this cause/need do you care most about?**

Examples:

a) Education:
— Adult Education
— High School Dropouts
— Illiteracy
— Job Retraining
— English as a Second Language
— Elementary Schools
— Day Care
— University Trustee
— Legislation

b) Social Services/Welfare:
— Mental Health Clinics
— Homeless/Housing
— Welfare Mothers' Rights
— Abused Women/Children
— Criminal Justice
— Hunger/Nutrition
— Abortion

2. **Determine what programs already exist in your community to address this need:**

a) Check with an information and referral agency.

b) Look through a community resources directory or the telephone directory.

c) Check with your local Volunteer Center, United Way, Chamber of Commerce, American Red Cross, etc.

3. **If programs currently exist:**

Request an interview to see what their present volunteer needs are, and to see if what they need matches what you want to share in skills, time, or money. If there's a match, you are on your way to making a difference that matters—to you, the organization, and those in need.

4. **If a program does not exist and you feel strongly that something needs to be done:**

a) Explore the extent of the need with professionals who work in that general category (i.e. education, welfare, health, church). Are clients they work with falling through the cracks in the system? If so, how many, and what would help? (Be sure to ask some clients these same questions.)

b) Ask the professionals if they know of any other communities that have exemplary programs that might be helpful resources. What are the national organizations that deal with this cause? Check your library for the excellent reference book by Sue Vineyard and Steve McCurley, *Resource Directory for Volunteer Programs,* or write to VOLUNTEER: The National Center, 1111 N. 19th St., Suite 500, Arlington, Virginia 22209, for information.

c) Establish a small planning group of individuals who share the same deep concern about this particular need. At this stage, look for both innovators and good organizers—you'll need creative ideas and the people who know how to carry them out. One way to recruit this group is to have a human interest story in the newspaper or on television or radio, telling about the need and what kind of people you are trying to recruit.

d) When you are ready to begin, try out your ideas as a pilot program. Monitor the plan and activities, make necessary adjustments, and assess the results. This should be done before too much publicity, red tape, and bureaucratic sanction is involved.

e) If it works, dare to go for it! Enthusiastically recruit money, volunteers, and community support. That is how most ideas that make a difference become a reality.

f) Be realistic about the amount of time, dedication, and just plain hard work it takes to start something new. Keep your mission clearly before you and the volunteers who help you. It is mission that motivates people. A helpful resource is the book *Starting and Running a Nonprofit Organization*, by Joan Hummel.

The Three Key Elements

What this plan clearly points out is that making a significant difference in a cause you care about involves three elements:

1) **Caring deeply about a cause**

2) **Investing hard work and follow-through**

3) **Daring to risk**

I have already discussed number one, so let me share some stories to illustrate the other two.

There is a story about Will Rogers who, during World War I, supposedly had this suggestion for getting rid of German submarines:

> All we have to do is heat up the Atlantic to 212 ° F. Then the subs will have to surface and we can pick them off one by one. Now, somebody's going to want to know how to warm up the ocean. Well, I'm not going to worry about that. It's a matter of detail, and I'm a policy-maker.

What a true illustration of the ivory tower thinker who

only dreams the big ideas and never deals with the hard, day-to-day practicality required to make it work. As the saying goes, "Be wary of the man who urges action in which he himself incurs no risk."

One of my favorite Charlie Brown stories beautifully illustrates the third element—risk:

> Charlie Brown was in his backyard practicing with his bow and arrow one day. He would pull the string back as far as he could and let the arrow fly into the back fence. Then he'd run over to the fence and draw a target around the arrow.

> Several hours later, Lucy showed up. "That's no way to target practice!" she screamed. "You're s'posed to draw the target first and then shoot at it." "I know that, Lucy," said Charlie, "but if you do it my way—you never miss!"

To start anything new takes courage, perseverance, and the willingness to risk. As M. Scott Peck observed, "We learn what is significantly new only through adventure . . . however, going into the unknown is invariably frightening."

One of the most rewarding experiences I have ever had was helping to start the Boulder County Volunteer and Information Center. Yet, I've probably never worked harder in my entire life. All of us who were involved experienced tremendous satisfaction as we began to see that real people who needed help were connected day after day with caring people who were willing and able to give it. We were all making a significant difference in our community and we knew it. The exciting part was, we were just ordinary people. But we all cared deeply about a cause, we acted on that concern, and we made our community a better place. You can do the same!

People Volunteering for Causes

Let me share some stories of other people and organizations who are making a real difference in their communities. To help you sort through them and find those concerns that might speak most directly to you, I have organized them into various categories. These are only a few examples of the thousands of ways in which ordinary (and some extraordinary) people are involved in causes they believe in.

LITERACY

First Lady Barbara Bush

Since President Bush's inauguration in January 1989, dozens of magazines, newspapers, and television talk shows have focused attention on this remarkable woman. In my opinion, she has brought more positive publicity to the cause of volunteerism than any other public figure in the past 20 years. Why? Because she has "walked the talk" as a life-long volunteer herself. Her personal story and philosophy of volunteering was the centerpiece of the July 10, 1989 issue of *Newsweek*, which devoted 10 pages to today's volunteers. In that article, Mrs. Bush talked about inheriting the value of community involvement from her parents. "We just grew up knowing that's what you did." So when her children were growing up, she did what so many mothers did and volunteered for everything from Little League to the March of Dimes. Still other, very personal and meaningful involvements came later:

- She worked at the Sloan-Kettering Cancer Center in New York and Hospice in Washington D.C., in response to the loss of their four-year-old daughter to leukemia in 1953.

- She worked as a volunteer in soup kitchens and shelters for the homeless.

Her special cause, however, is literacy:

> In the last 10 years she has personally visited over 500 literacy programs in libraries, schools, day-care centers, housing projects, and shelters. The privately-funded Barbara Bush Foundation for Family Literacy supports reading programs around the country.[3]

People do make the most difference in causes they care about personally and passionately. In the *Parade* magazine article, "Everything Would Be Better if More People Could Read," (May 21, 1989), Mrs. Bush said her fight against illiteracy began 25 years ago. And it is the startling reality that 23 million Americans are considered functionally illiterate and another 35 million Americans are semi-literate that led her to decide what cause she would highlight as First Lady:

> I spent a whole summer thinking about what would help the most people possible. And it suddenly occurred to me that every single thing I worry about—things like teen pregnancies, the breakup of families, drugs, AIDS, the homeless—everything would be better if more people could read, write and understand.[4]

And so, this outstanding volunteer has become a symbol, advocate, and spokesperson for the nation's 80 million volunteers.

Literacy Volunteers of America

This outstanding program involves more than 60,000 tutors and students in more than 300 programs in 35 states. (The number of students and volunteers has doubled in the last two years.)

How did it begin? With a single person, Ruth Johnson Colvin, in Syracuse, New York, in 1962. Colvin became very concerned after reading an article that said more than 11,000 people in her community could not read simple directions or forms. She worked with Syracuse University to develop materials to teach volunteer tutors motivation and teaching techniques. Then she recruited and trained members of her own church women's group as tutors.

The program was so successful that other communities asked her to conduct workshops to help them. She did, and this early training still forms the basis of the training for the now-nationwide organization that emerged. Literacy Volunteers of America has now helped more than 100,000 people learn to read. Colvin continues to tutor and research new ways of teaching and training volunteers and program directors. She received one of the President's Volunteer Action Awards in 1987 for her contribution to the country through volunteerism.

For information on this outstanding program, write to: Literacy Volunteers of America, Inc., 5795 Widewaters Parkway, Syracuse, NY 13214-1846, or call (315) 445-8000.

SCHOOL DROPOUTS

I Have a Dream Foundation

I once attended a national conference where one of the keynote speakers was an exceptional man by the name of Eugene Lang. Lang is the founder of the I Have a Dream Foundation. This was his story about how it began:

In 1981, Lang, a multi-millionaire businessman, had been asked to address the graduating class of 61 sixth-graders in a poverty-stricken Harlem neighborhood. He knew the school well, as he had graduated from there 53 years earlier. He also knew the dropout rate for inner-city minority kids was 75 percent or more.

"This is your first graduation—just the perfect time to dream—dream of what to be, the kind of life you wish to build. And believe in that dream," he started his speech. "Always remember, each dream is important because it is your dream, it is your future. And it is worth working for. To make this dream come true you must study. You must attend junior high school, high school, and college. You must go to college, stay in school and I'll . . ." He paused, and in an instant of inspiration, he added, "I will give you each a college scholarship." Which he did—to the 49 kids who stayed in school.

This was the start of a program that matches one adult volunteer with one graduating fifth- or sixth-grader. The students are called "dreamers" and the adults working with them one-on-one provide financial and personal support to that student all the way through high school and often college. They are available to the "dreamers" at any time to help deal with the system, encourage parent support, and develop self-esteem and competency in their student.

Does it make a difference? The dropout rate of "dreamers" in this program is 5 percent, as opposed to 75 percent. There are more than 4,000 students in the program and two-thirds of them opt for college. I Have a Dream programs are spreading to many other cities across the country.

For information on starting such a program, write: I Have a Dream Foundation, 31 W. 34th Street, New York, New York 10001.

HOMELESS/HOUSING

There are a vast number of desperately needed and worthwhile projects across this country that have been established by community groups, religious organizations, and coalitions to deal with our nation's rapidly growing problem of homelessness. So many articles have been written and television specials have been produced examining this national tragedy that I will not discuss the causes of the problem. Rather, I would like to highlight a remarkable program that has focused on meeting more than just the basic needs of the poor and often homeless elderly.

Sarah's Circle, Washington, D.C.

This program is located in our nation's capitol—a city which has increasingly become a contrast of the powerful and powerless, the rich and the poor, the law-makers and the disenfranchised.

Sarah's Circle began as the concern (actually the "call") of the well-known author, Elizabeth O'Connor of Washington, D.C. In describing the problems of the elderly poor, O'Connor says:

> More devastating than ill health is loneliness. Denied work, and cut off from any real involvement in the world they must live in, the forgotten poor spend their long days in dismal, low-rent rooming houses or are forced onto the streets.

Her journey in struggling with this very urgent need is beautifully described in her book, *Cry Pain, Cry Hope.* Sarah's Circle is now a reality. It was once a 40-year-old dilapidated inner-city building that was bought by Jubilee Housing, Inc., a nonprofit organization. It was renovated primarily by volunteers, many of whom are now residents.

In defining her vision for Sarah's Circle, O'Connor says:

> A sense of belonging, the safety and security of a close-knit neighborhood, a good work to do, an opportunity to participate in creating a caring community of all ages and backgrounds—these experiences are at the heart of Sarah's Circle . . . it is designed to demonstrate that old age is rich with possibilities . . . each person, no matter how old, has an important creative work to do.

Sarah's Circle is governed, and to a large part staffed by the residents. They also provide some of the dramas and seminars in their educational program, interact with the children of the Children's House nearby, and provide support and counsel to young low-income mothers and their babies in the neighborhood.

It works without any federal subsidies, deriving funds from churches, corporations, foundations, and individuals. Even the residents give what they can. For example, Beulah Rivers sells used clothes on the corner every weekend she can and gives all the proceeds (averaging $150 per week) to the building development fund. These people are definitely givers as well as receivers.

As their brochure states, "the message of Sarah's Circle is that nothing we can envision is impossible. The old can be empowered for the ushering in of a new world where clean and safe space, good food, health care, and self-esteem are assured to every human being."

They not only believe this—but are putting it into action! This project can be duplicated in other places. Write to: Sarah's Circle, 2552 17th Street, Washington, DC 20009.

Miracle on 27th Street, Milwaukee, Wisconsin

Another exemplary program dealing with the problem of low-cost housing is called Miracle on 27th Street. This project involved the large not-for-profit Lutheran fraternal insurance company, Aid Association for Lutherans (AAL); a Jewish philanthropist; businesses; churches; and people of all shapes, sizes, ages, and faiths. What was common among them was a desire to help those less fortunate and to revitalize a central city neighborhood. The Jewish philanthropist donated four buildings in need of renovation to a local church-sponsored foundation. AAL provided dozens of their members as volunteers and a $147,000 grant to refurbish the exteriors of the buildings. Businesses and churches "adopted" individual apartments and restored them. This involved hundreds of volunteer hours and approximately $2,000 per apartment.

Now that the complex is completed, it provides decent, affordable housing at rents ranging from $210 to $350 for 32 families. Edward Ruen, executive director of the foundation sponsoring the project said, "I haven't seen a project of this magnitude where there has been so much of a concentration of volunteer activity and authentic caring and gift-giving. It captured people's imaginations. The bottom line: people felt their contribution would serve a need in the future."[5]

Habitat for Humanity

This is one of the best-known programs for building and renovating low-income housing. Former President Jimmy Carter and his wife Rosalynn are active volunteers in this endeavor, which has renovated more than 2,000 homes for people with little or no money. This ecumenical program, which was founded in 1976, secures land, seeks building material donations and financial contributions, and then builds homes in partnership with the homeowner families. Habitat for Humanity now has 324 affiliates in the U.S. and involves more than 35,000 volunteers. There are also Habitat-sponsored projects in Canada, Australia, and 25 developing countries.

To receive additional information on this 1989 President's Volunteer Action Award-winning program, write to: Habitat for Humanity, Habitat and Church Streets, Americus, Georgia 31709-3498.

Shelters for the Homeless

There are local shelters for the homeless in almost every community, and they are funded and staffed primarily by volunteers. It is an opportunity for people to reach out to help those in need in very concrete and vitally-needed ways. Watch your local newspapers for appeals for volunteers or see your Volunteer Center, Salvation Army, or religious organization to find out how you can help. This is certainly a cause that needs the creative energy of volunteers, not only to help meet the current need, but to help find long-range solutions for the problem.

HUNGER

The Senior Gleaners, Sacramento, California

This incredible organization was founded in 1976 by Homer Fahrner, a twice-retired businessman. He was deeply concerned because he saw people going hungry and at the same time, food going to waste. He wanted to do something about this inequity, so he put his ideas in a senior citizens' weekly newspaper and asked for 20 people who might be interested in exploring the idea. He received 200 calls. Thirty-eight people attended a meeting, and eight said "let's do it" and they went to work. They contacted farmers who had food they couldn't sell due to size, shape, color, or surplus. They found many who were willing to let them take unused food to distribute free to their senior members. Six years after they began, the Gleaners distributed more than five million pounds of food products to more than 1,600 members. They now also "glean" food from supermarkets and canneries, and redistribute it to other food banks and local charities.[6] Although this organization claims to be the largest gleaning operation in the U.S., there are hundreds of similar programs across the country. Contact the state Farm Bureau or 4-H and Extension Office in your county to find out how to become involved.

"Daddy" Bruce Randolph

At 88 years of age, Daddy Bruce, as he is affectionately known, has fed the hungry of Denver, Colorado, for more than 30 years. Every Thanksgiving he recruits volunteers to help prepare and serve dinner to those who would otherwise not eat at all. He provides the food and the caring. As owner of Daddy Bruce's Bar-B-Q, a long-time Denver restaurant, Daddy Bruce is a simple, unassuming man who has seen a need—a cause—and has done something about it. In addition to his free Thanksgiving dinners, he offers food, clothes, Christmas trees, and toys during the holidays. He's been called a one-man social service agency—seeing to it that the donations he receives are given to those in need.[7]

SERIOUSLY-ILL CHILDREN

Make-A-Wish Foundation

This group works with youth under 18 who have life-threatening diseases. Its sole mission is to make childhood fantasies come true. It may be a trip to Disneyland, a chance to meet a television or sports star, or even something as simple as a new bed. There are now 63 chapters in the United States. Hundreds of volunteers are involved in fund raising as well as actively working with the children and their families. As Michele Atkins, executive director of the Western Pennsylvania chapter explains, "We have a chance, for a day or two, to take away all the confusion and fear and despair a child is feeling and leave nothing behind but joy and promise."[8]

The Ronald McDonald Houses

These houses provide the families of seriously-ill children inexpensive places to stay during a child's treatment at regional children's hospitals. The first house was founded in Philadelphia in 1974 by Jim Murray, then general manager of the Philadelphia Eagles; Dr. Audrey Evans, a pediatric oncologist; and Fred Hill, an Eagles tight-end and father of a young child with leukemia. The 100-plus Ronald McDonald houses are now operated as locally-owned, non-profit corporations with little or no paid staff. They involve more than 5,000 volunteers and have housed more than one million people.

Volunteer "Baby-Holders"

In New York, Washington D.C., and several other U.S. cities, there are hospitals that have an extremely innovative volunteer program. They have brought together "boarder babies" (infants who are born to drug-addicted mothers) and volunteer "baby-holders." And, surprisingly, more and more of the volunteers involved are men. In an article about the program at St. Luke's Hospital in New York, it was noted that among the male volunteers is a transplanted Londoner, a former New York city police officer, an international banker, a professional model, a lawyer, a retired security guard, and an education consultant with a Ph.D. The ages range from mid-twenties to late-sixties and the only thing these volunteers have in common is an uncommon love of babies. Most of the babies are suffering withdrawal, and since their mothers are not there to hold them, the volunteers provide the love and cuddling the infants so desperately need.

If you want to start a Baby-Holder Program in your area and want more information, write to: Virginia Crosby, St. Luke's-Roosevelt Hospital Center, Dept. P, 428 W. 59th Street, New York, New York 10019, Attention: Volunteer Department.[9]

CRIME/DRUGS

The Guardian Angels

Curtis Sliwa founded the Guardian Angels, a volunteer nonprofit civilian patrol whose primary mission is to prevent urban crime. Many Angels are under age 21; many are black and Hispanic. They patrol subways, provide escort services to the elderly, distribute food, and advocate the prevention of drug use. The nearly 5,000 members are now in 51 American and 4 Canadian cities. They raise money locally, and no one is salaried. "The value of volunteer service, and it's not just a cliché, it is the most valuable work you can possibly do," Sliwa said. "It is one of the few areas you can instantly see results . . . most of the problems in the community are problems that we in the community can deal with, ninety-nine percent of them. Absolutely."

Discussing why he got involved in this difficult type of volunteering, Sliwa said:

> I think it was just a process of gnawing a little bit each time, having heard of the crime, having seen the victim, having traveled through a neighborhood that was deteriorating and crime-ravaged, and listening to the political and police officials, the so-called know-it-alls, tell us don't go downtown, travel in a group of a thousand, don't, don't, don't, don't—literally reshape our whole life because of the problems of crime. And I just said, no way—there's got to be something different. And it essentially got down to somebody had to do something that wasn't violent, that utilized the laws that already existed, that developed the positive role model effect that I believe is the crux of the problem, and did so in a multiracial way so as to embrace all communities and not just the few and the chosen.[10]

PANDAA (Parents Association to Neutralize Drug and Alcohol Abuse), Fairfax County, Virginia

The founder and leader of this very active and concerned group of parents is Joyce Tobias. Joyce shared with me that the compelling impetus for her starting the group in 1980 was discovering that two of her own seven children were using drugs. She and her husband desperately sought help and information and found little available. So she researched parent intervention programs and gathered teen substance abuse statistics from around the country. Then, with the cooperation of the principal, she called a meeting of high school parents in her wealthy Washington, D.C. suburban area. More than 120 people came to the meeting. She had sign-up sheets for people to identify committees or work areas they would volunteer for, and almost everyone signed up to help. They became a formal nonprofit organization within six weeks and got to work on a variety of projects.

Their first priority was to learn about the problem of

youth and drugs, so they held parent awareness meetings. They also worked hard to educate principals, teachers, and school board and city officials. Joyce then began to publish a newsletter (PANDAA) which has become a very powerful education and advocacy tool, not only in her own community, but around the country. Other projects have been a "parents' listening ear" service; and a court watch program, where volunteers monitor drug-related cases and send statistics to newspapers, legislators, etc. The school board approved close to 30 recommendations regarding drug and alcohol use in schools put forward by a PANDAA/school-sponsored task force. Joyce has authored three books: *Kids and Drugs*, *Schools and Drugs*, and *Courts and Drugs*.

For information on this outstanding program, write: PANDAA, 4111 Watkins Trail, Annandale, Virginia 22003.

ELDERLY

National Association for the Jewish Poor

Louis Leeder cofounded the National Association for the Jewish Poor in 1979 to provide services to poor, elderly, and homebound Jewish people in South Bronx, Harlem, Brownsville, and East New York. By 1986, when he received a President's Volunteer Action Award, this young man had involved 900 trained high school and college students who served more than 1,500 seniors each month. These volunteers collected and distributed food, electric heaters, fans, and blankets; provided daily kosher meals at two synagogues; and conducted intergenerational programs including singing, movies, and lectures. They also provided emergency hot lines and made daily reassurance calls.

Meals on Wheels

Meals on Wheels programs offer low-cost meals to the homebound in almost every community, and are in constant need of volunteer drivers. Many employed people have found it possible to undertake this assignment on their lunch breaks. Look in your telephone directory for the number to call if you want to help.

American Red Cross

The American Red Cross has numerous programs serving the elderly, such as transportation and shopping services, and telephone reassurance, all of which involve volunteers. Give your local chapter a call.

Magic Me

Magic Me is an innovative approach to working with people in nursing homes. Its founder is Kathy Levin, whose inspiring story is in *Local Heroes*, by Bill Berkowitz. Levin tried volunteering in a nursing home in college and was overwhelmed by how many volunteers in the home were bored. It seemed apparent to her that they didn't want to be there, so were not giving their jobs much energy. After several years of trying out some of her own ideas on how to bring joy into volunteering—and to nursing home patients—she settled on the Magic Me idea. She started her program in Baltimore, where she recruits and carefully trains preteen volunteers. Wearing bright T-shirts and big smiles, they make friends with the patients, teach them to dance, write poetry, play basketball, sing—almost any activity that is interactive and fun. This program has become so successful that CBS did a special television feature on it, and requests are pouring in from across the country from others who would like to replicate it. Magic Me has done as much for the youth who volunteer as for the patients. It helps them develop a new way of looking at themselves and their own lives and most especially, their fears and attitudes about aging.[11] This program is now in 20 U.S. cities, Paris, and London. For information on starting a Magic Me program in your area, write to: Magic Me, 611 Park Avenue, Suite 6, Baltimore, Maryland 21201, or call (301) 837-0900.

HANDICAPPED

The Cooperative Wilderness Outdoor Group

The Cooperative Wilderness Outdoor Group was formed in 1981 by Tom Whitaker, a veteran outdoorsman who had his right foot amputated after an automobile accident. This group has taken hundreds of disabled adventurers on such exciting outings as dog sledding in Wyoming and river rafting in Idaho. "If you turn people's minds from sympathy (toward the disabled) to admiration," Whittaker says, "the more negative feelings evaporate."[12]

Many communities offer opportunities for volunteers to work with the handicapped through programs like Special Olympics, handicapped skiing and swimming programs, and Braille transcribing and reading for the blind. Check with your local Volunteer Center for opportunities.

Volunteers for Medical Engineering

This is a group of engineers whose goal is to help public and charitable agencies assist the disabled through the use of engineering expertise. They have developed such wonders as an automatic door opener for wheelchair users, a hands-free telephone, a fully electronic wheelchair, and a chin-operated device to help a cerebral-palsied youngster to communicate.[13]

SELF-HELP GROUPS

In the past decade, more and more people have started to look away from institutions for help and are looking toward themselves. One of the most common ways in which people have done this is through self-help groups which offer advice and support. In fact, there are over 500,000 such groups today.

These groups are usually run by volunteers, and the people who join them help one another with a mutual problem or concern. The most well-known is Alcoholics

Anonymous, but many newspapers have weekly listings of hundred of others. A few examples from my community's Sunday newspaper are:

• Smokers Anonymous
• Narcotics Anonymous
• Workaholics Anonymous
• Single Fathers Support Group
• Overeaters Anonymous
• Parkinson's Support Group
• Alzheimer's Disease Support Group
• Cancer Support Group
• Siblings & Adult Children of the Mentally Ill
• Stroke Club
• Caregivers' Support Group
• Infant Loss Support Group

This is often a way people can address a cause that they are personally affected by—not only offering mutual support, but also advocating for changes needed in legislation and public education.

These are just a small sample of the causes people are caring about. My hope is that these stories might inspire you to follow whatever your dream might be to make this a better world. As these people have made a difference—so can you!

> *I believe that the transforming movement that raises the quality of any institution, large or small, begins with the initiative of one individual person—no matter how large the institution or how substantial the movement.*
>
> *—John Gardner*

—•7•—

Sharing Your
Lifetime Experience

*The most beautiful people I have known are those
who have known defeat, known suffering, known
struggle, known loss, and have found their way out
of the depths. Those people have an appreciation, a
sensitivity, and an understanding of life that fills
them with compassion, gentleness, and a deep
loving concern . . . Beautiful people do not just
happen.*

—Historian Ray Nichols

One of my good friends, Arlene Schindler, has a
philosophy of life that I admire and have come to
believe in: *Nothing is irrelevant!* She has changed careers
approximately every five years because, "there is so much
to learn and so many new skills waiting to be developed."

In her 60-plus years, just a few of her challenges have
included being a teacher and then principal in an inner-city
Detroit high school in her twenties; serving as one of the
original Peace Corps trainers, ultimately traveling in more

than 100 countries around the world; becoming director of training for The National Center for Voluntary Action (predecessor to VOLUNTEER: The National Center); and being a national executive for Women in Community Service and Prison Fellowship. She is now with Special Olympics.

Her personal adventures have been as challenging as her work. She has traveled over the Lapland by reindeer, taken the Trans-Siberian Railroad across the Soviet Union, lived among cannibals in New Guinea, played the tuba in a philharmonic orchestra (even though she is only 5'2"), and informally adopted and provided college educations for more than a dozen young people from around the world—and then sent them back to their own countries as valuable resources.

Arlene's zest for living and her ability to enjoy the fullest array of experiences possible are contagious. She believes that nothing one ever does or learns is irrelevant—it is incorporated into our personal bank of knowledge and wisdom that enriches our next experience. To me, she epitomizes the true life-long learner. She eagerly anticipates retirement as yet another opportunity to use what she has learned in still new and different ways as a volunteer.

It is with this notion in mind that I approach the topic of volunteering as a way of sharing what you have spent a lifetime acquiring: your own unique set of skills, knowledge, and wisdom. Someone once observed, "Knowledge is knowing facts; wisdom is knowing what to do with the facts you know." I will be focusing on the retirement years in this chapter and will include the rapidly growing group of early retirees, because this has become a new national phenomenon.

A United Way study on volunteerism in the 1990s indicated that:[1]

■ In 1975—75 percent of men ages 55-64 were in the paid work force.

- In 1984—68.5 percent of men ages 55-64 were in the paid work force.

- By 1995—62.6 percent of men ages 55-64 will be in the paid work force.

These figures represent a decrease of almost *13 percent* in the number of men ages 55-64 in the paid work force from 1975 to 1995. In other words, as the years progress, fewer and fewer men will be staying in the paid work force until age 64. What will they be doing?

These trends also affect women, not only because more of them will be retiring from the workforce at an earlier age, but also because homemakers will be living much longer after the children leave the nest. The average life span of Americans has increased by 35 years over the last century. So, this important group of people is increasing dramatically.

A Healthy Attitude is the Key

Retirement at any age is a major life transition for both men and women. But, the transition of retirement can be a time for new, exciting experiences as well as a broadening and sharing of skills and wisdom. As Gail Sheehy observed in her book *Passages*:

> With each passage from one stage of human growth to the next we, too, must shed a protective structure. We are left exposed and vulnerable—but also yeasty and embryonic again, capable of stretching in ways we hadn't known before.[2]

I discussed earlier the importance of attitude. I can think of no time when attitude is more important than in retirement and aging. There seems to be a very clear distinction between those who age gracefully and those who resentfully see it as one of life's dirty tricks. In the first instance, getting older seems to be experienced for what it is—a natural progression of life itself. Retirement opens the door to new adventures and challenges. Those who age grudgingly and bitterly are often those who only look backward at what they feel they have lost—instead of forward to new and different possibilities. As Jennifer James says in her book, *Windows*:

> We're all getting older. There are rewards and tradeoffs, but there is also loss. Pretending it's not there can leave us unable to make the transition, and unexpectedly depressed. This is a culture that rewards youth and beauty, and it is unlikely to change anytime soon . . . Having laid out that truth, I can counter it with the incredible pleasures that come with the deepening of self that is part of long life-experience: self knowledge, stronger values, a sense of personal honor, awareness of competence, independence, freedom from competition, and an identity separate from the opposite sex—all are wonders of getting older.

James states that research indicates that if a person's health remains good, their happiest years are the 60s and 70s. She believes the key to that happiness is running your own life at last. "If you continue to live by others' expectations or your culture's definition of your worth, aging will be hell. Put some energy into deciding what you want to do."[3]

Since attitude is such an important factor in how we age, let me share with you some thought-provoking quotations:[4]

As long as you live, keep learning how to live.

—Seneca

Life's a great big canvas; throw all the paint on it you can.

—Danny Kaye

Don't forget until it's too late that the business of life is not business, but living.

—B. C. Forbes

All men should strive to learn before they die what they are running from and to and why.

—James Thurber

Retirement at 65 is ridiculous! When I was 65 I still had pimples.

—George Burns

Take care that old age does not wrinkle your spirit even more than your face.

—Michel de Montaigne

I'm 78 years old and nobody ever knows what to call me—Senior Citizen, or Older American, or what. Do you know what I like to be called? Chronologically gifted!

—Workshop Participant

Volunteering is Good for Your Health

Those of us involved in the world of volunteerism have known for years that volunteering can positively affect the attitudes of older people. When a person's energy is focused on helping others—rather than concentrating on their own aches, pains, and isolation—new vigor and enthusiasm result. The need to be needed is a primary motivator for human beings, and this need does not diminish with age.

In the early '70s, the Boulder Volunteer and Information Center sought to reach out and recruit the lonely and isolated seniors in our community as volunteers. These were the people who were still in their own homes or apartments, but had withdrawn from almost all social interaction. They lived their lives primarily in front of the television set. Their contact with others was often confined to the Meals-on-Wheels volunteer and the Visiting Nurse. The experts on aging told us that the next step for them would be a nursing home. We felt that we might prolong their independent life styles if we could get them involved with others again.

We realized that the usual volunteer assignments were not appropriate for this particular group. Their primary need was to socialize in a safe environment, use arthritic limbs again, and recapture a sense of self-worth that comes from doing something useful. As a result, we organized a biweekly volunteer group at the local Red Cross. We had the Visiting Nurses and Meals-on-Wheels staff introduce us to their homebound clients. Then we invited them to come to the group and see if they liked it. We provided transportation, refreshments, and worthwhile group projects (such as making tray favors for day-care centers, health kits for the health department, or mailings for agencies). Gradually, the people became comfortable with socializing while they worked and within a few months they wanted to meet twice a week.

The greatest joy was when some of these older persons asked to go with us when we delivered their handiwork so they could see who benefitted from their efforts. I will never forget the day one of these wonderful women went with me to a day-care center. A little boy tugged on her skirt and asked if he could sit on her lap and hear a story. She beamed and said, "Of course—I've got a good lap to sit on!" After that she became a regular volunteer at the day-care center. We had a significant number of others who had similar "graduations" to more individual volunteer endeavors.

Another example of the positive effects volunteering can

have on seniors was a woman named Lucy, who we interviewed in a retirement home in Boulder. The director of the
home had told us that Lucy was becoming more and more
lethargic and reclusive, and her appearance was becoming
slovenly. She was having difficulty finding a reason to get
out of bed in the morning—so often, she didn't. As we visited
with Lucy, we asked her if she had ever worked outside the
home during her marriage. She said she had been a receptionist in an office for many years and had really enjoyed it.
We told her that the YMCA in our city was in desperate need
of volunteers to staff the information desk during the day,
and asked her if she'd like to give it a try. She hesitated for
awhile, saying she really wasn't sure she could do that
anymore. Finally, she agreed to try it one afternoon a week.
Soon she was not only serving as the receptionist three days
a week, but she had a new hairstyle and wardrobe and was
walking the six blocks to and from the YMCA. The director
of the retirement home was absolutely amazed.

Lucy was a perfect example of what William Hazlett
meant when he said: "Let not the cloud sit upon your brow;
let not the canker sink into your heart. Look up, laugh loud,
talk big, keep the colour in your cheek and the fire in your
eye, adorn your person, maintain your health and your
beauty . . ."

Yes, volunteering does have a decided effect on one's
psychological and emotional well-being. But even more exciting, there is now sound research proving that volunteering prolongs life expectancy and improves the physical
well-being of older persons as well.

In the March 1988 issue of *American Health* magazine,
there was an article by Eileen Rockefeller Growald and Allan
Luks, entitled "The Immunity of Samaritans: Beyond Self."
Epidemiologist James House and his colleagues at the
University of Michigan's Survey Research Center studied
2,700 older people in Tecumseh, Michigan. For more than a
decade, they examined how social relationships affected the
health of the subjects and concluded that helping other

people results in real physical and psychological benefits.

The article reported that, in this study, doing regular volunteer work, *more than any other activity*, dramatically increased life expectancy. The difference was especially significant for men. The article noted, "Men who did no volunteer work were two-and-one-half times as likely to die during the study as men who volunteered at least once a week."

They also referred to other similar studies being done at Yale, the University of California, Johns Hopkins University, the National Institute of Mental Health, and Ohio State University. These studies all seem to indicate that doing good for others through volunteering is not only beneficial to a person's nervous system but the immune system as well.

The article concluded:

> Just as people now exercise and watch their diets to protect their health, they may soon scrape peeling paint from their elderly neighbor's house, collect money for the March of Dimes, campaign for a nuclear freeze, teach illiterates how to read or clean up trash from a public park—all for the same self-protective reason.[5]

This is dramatic proof that people who volunteer do indeed get back more than they give!

Sharing Expertise and Experience

The major theme of this chapter is the importance of valuing and using the experience it has taken a lifetime to acquire. Sometimes we forget who the real experts are, as the following true story illustrates:

> The elevator at the El Cortez Hotel in San Diego couldn't handle the traffic. The experts—engineers and architects—were called in. They concluded that they could put another elevator in by cutting a hole in each

floor and installing the motor for the new elevator in the basement. The plans were drawn up. Everything was in order. The architect and engineer came into the lobby discussing it. The janitor, who had been with the hotel many years, heard them say they were going to chop holes in the floor.

The janitor said, "That's going to make a mess." The engineer said, "Of course. But we'll get help for you, don't worry." The janitor replied, "You'll have to close the hotel for a while." "Well, if we have to close the hotel for awhile, we'll close it. We can't possibly survive without another elevator."

The janitor leaned on his mop and said, "Do you know what I would do if I were you?" The architect arrogantly asked, "What?" "I'd build the elevator on the outside." The architect and engineer just looked at each other.

They built the elevator on the outside—the first time in the history of architecture that an elevator was built on the outside of a building.[6]

One of the great contributions that volunteers of all ages bring to organizations is their unique perspectives and solutions, ones that even the experts often miss because they are too close to the situation or problem.

Agencies and organizations that integrate volunteers properly have a new and exciting opportunity to tap into enormous expertise today, since people are retiring younger with better health and a wider array of skills. One of the greatest challenges for managers is to utilize this rich resource and not be threatened by the fact that a retiree's experience and expertise may in some instances surpass that of their paid staff.

Let me illustrate this with a true story. Joseph Shapiro

was a newly-retired clothing manufacturer from New York City. He decided he wanted to volunteer, so he visited several volunteer agencies in the city. In each case, they suggested only non-challenging "paper pushing" jobs to him. Then he talked to Winnie Brown, the executive director of the New York City Mayor's Voluntary Action Center. When Winnie learned of his expertise in clothing manufacturing, she said, "How would you like to head up our efforts to provide clothing to the homeless in New York?" Now that was a challenge worthy of the man, and he accepted it. In just three years, under Shapiro's leadership, the clothing bank solicited and obtained donations of more than two million items of *new* clothing (valued at well over $8 million) from 600 clothing manufacturers nationally. The clothing was distributed to more than 250 programs serving the homeless in New York City. Mr. Shapiro passed away in April of 1989, but what a legacy of service he left. This program received one of the President's Volunteer Action Awards in 1989.

How Retirees are Helping

Thousands of people over the age of 60 volunteer. Let me relate a few examples of what they are doing:

—Jane Koerber, age 78, has volunteered at the American Red Cross in Denver, Colorado, since 1985. A retired nurse, she has worked in the Home Nursing Program, AIDS education program, and has also been active with the Denver Red Cross Disaster Action Team. She is available at a moment's notice to help victims of local disasters, including house fires and other emergencies. She is also a member of the national Red Cross Disaster Services Human Resources Program and works as a nurse at disasters around the country. "If you've made someone feel a little better, it gives you a good, warm feeling," Koerber said. "I enjoy volunteering for the Red Cross because I like to think maybe I've helped somebody.

Everyone should have a hobby or something to do—being active keeps you young. I've never worried that each day I'm one day older and have a little more gray in my hair—you have to live for today."

—Ethel Williams from Paterson, New Jersey, is a retired teacher living in the city's poorest neighborhood. She provides counseling and crisis intervention assistance to her neighbors and operates a food pantry out of her home.

—Richard Stair, a retired railroad laborer with 42 years of service, has turned his long-time hobby of scouring library stacks for railroad literature into a satisfying volunteer job. He knew the problem that library employees have keeping materials in proper order on the shelves, so he has become a regular volunteer "shelf-reader" for the University of Illinois Library at Urbana-Champaign. "You get an unusual sense of accomplishment when you find a volume that isn't where it should be," he said. "It's like finding a lost treasure."

—A participant in one of my church volunteerism workshops shared with me that she was a newly-retired personnel executive for the State of Alaska. Her pastor had asked her to consider becoming the coordinator of volunteers for her congregation, so she came to my workshop to discover what that would entail. At the end of the event she came to me and excitedly said, "I can't wait to start this job. I now see that I'll be able to use all of my personnel skills and help my church at the same time!"

—Jack Glover, a 74-year-old retired graphic artist, has worked as a volunteer for over a decade to develop a trail along the North Umpqua River in Oregon. He spearheaded the formation of the Umpqua Trails Council, comprised of 11 trail-user groups with more than 300 members. Glover uses his technical layout experience to route the trail and place flag markers. Then he supervises other volunteers in developing the trail (removing large windfall trees and underbrush, building bridges, etc.). He has personally volunteered more than 40 percent of the actual labor on the trail and in one year drove 5,000 miles on trail business. He was a 1987 recipient of the President's Volunteer Action Award.

—Frances Freeborn Pauley, 83, has been involved in social activism for more than 60 years. Frances began her social activism during the Depression when she set up a hot-lunch program for the DeKalb County schools. As president of a local chapter of the League of Women Voters in the '40s, she struck the bylaws clause limiting membership to whites. She was jailed in the '60s for working to desegregate schools and organizing interracial committees. In 1983, Frances founded the Georgia Poverty Rights Organization, a coalition of 1,500 activists and poor people. Her specific objective was to lobby the legislature, but her broader aim, she said, has been "to show poor people they counted." A great-grandmother, Frances believes, "It's just not fair the way some people have to suffer. You'd think I'd get toughened to it. Sometimes I think I can't stand the hurt."[7]

—Lorena Casey, age 75, retired from her job at a newspaper advertisement department in 1981, and decided to volunteer for a cause she cared about—shelters for battered women. As a child, Lorena often saw her father beating her mother, who stayed in the marriage for the sake of her children. Lorena now volunteers 50 hours a week for NEWS House for Battered Women in Kansas City. She answers the hot line (which goes directly to her apartment) and offers advice, gives information, and makes referrals. "You can't tell them what to do, they have to decide," Lorena says. "Lots of times they just want to talk to somebody who can tell them what options they have."[8]

—Chessie Harris, 84, of Huntsville, Alabama, has been mother to more than 800 disadvantaged youths for over 30 years. At a time when there were no other state facilities to care for homeless children, she and her late husband, George Harris, bought an acre of land, built a house, and began the Harris Home for Children. Since its founding in 1958, the Home has expanded to include the main facility, known as the "campus," and six satellite homes throughout Huntsville. With funding from United Way, Harris Home is structured on a family format. "We stress the family unit as a basis," Chessie said. "We are the parents of the children in the home, if you will." Throughout the years, Harris Home has managed to reclaim hundreds of children from starvation, neglect, and ignorance. In 1989, Chessie received a President's Volunteer Action Award for her outstanding human service contributions.[9]

—Maurice White, a 72-year-old bachelor who never had children, has been a school volunteer in Boston since 1983. He helps elementary school students with reading, writing, and arithmetic via the computer. A retired owner of a family hardware business, Maurice had never touched a computer prior to becoming a school volunteer, but after a few training sessions, he was ready to teach. Maurice signed up after hearing a radio spot about volunteering soon after he retired. "I was bored from just reading and taking walks," he said. "I see other retired people who work very hard to keep themselves busy. I don't have to do that; I know where I'm going every day."[10]

Volunteering as a Group Activity

One of the most devastating aspects of aging can be loneliness and isolation. As health problems develop and self-confidence wanes, it becomes easy to let the television or radio become the only contact with the outside world. So it is not unusual that people hope for a chance to socialize and interact with others while they volunteer. Even for more active people, it's often much more fun to do things together than alone. There are thousands of worthwhile group projects already established and well suited for social contact mixed with volunteering. Contact your local Retired Senior Volunteer Program (RSVP), American Red Cross, Volunteer Center, or Senior Citizen Center for suggestions. Following are a few examples of senior volunteer groups:

—The Telephone Pioneers of America have many volunteer projects across the country. In New York, for example, they annually involve more than 3,000 telecommunications employees and retirees in repairing 90,000 talking books and cassette machines for the blind. Another Pioneer group developed special soft balls (with sound) for children who are blind.

—The Ethnic Elder Program for Hispanic and African Seniors is located in Kenosha, Wisconsin. The Kenosha Voluntary Action Center started the program to help seniors with retirement, illness, and changed life circumstances. This program not only facilitates educational and recreational activities for its members, but arranges volunteer opportunities as well. Two of the leaders of the group are very enthusiastic about the results. Efrain Jaramillo was forced to retire because of illness: "I didn't feel like I was worth anything," he said, "so all day I would just look at the television . . ." When he was invited to join the Ethnic Elder Program, he became an active volunteer driver and is involved in other activities. "My life has changed," he said. "I'm happy now that I'm active and a part of the community. As a volunteer, I work for my heart, not for the money." And 69-year-old Oletha Harper found that when her husband died and she retired, volunteering became more important to her. "Just because we're retired doesn't mean we have to sit around and let the grass grow under our feet . . . forget about the soap operas and get out and do things . . . volunteering provided me the opportunity to develop my skills and personal growth."[11]

—**The California Grey Bears, Inc.,** of Santa Cruz, California, is a senior self-help organization. It manages a recycling plant and other profit-making enterprises that help fund a variety of services to seniors. One of their projects, called Operation Brown Bag, involved gathering and donating more than 65,000 pounds of food to more than 3,400 members. This program received a President's Volunteer Action Citation in 1988.

—**Amanda the Panda Volunteers** in Fort Lauderdale, Florida, was developed to involve senior women in teaching parenting skills to new mothers. This is a valuable service since 58 percent of the 14,200 babies born in Broward County, Florida, each year are to first-time parents, single mothers, and mothers under the age of 21. One group of senior volunteers (who are all in nursing homes) assembles packets of helpful parenting information. Another group of trained volunteers visits the new mothers in the hospital to deliver the packets and provide useful information about services. They even hold monthly "Panda Parties." This program received a President's Volunteer Action Award in 1985.

—**Programs like ACE, SCORE, and Executive Service Corps** are active in many parts of the country. These organizations are comprised of retired executives who are available to advise small businesses and nonprofit organizations on management and financial issues. (See Appendix B for more information on these organizations.)

—**Seattle, Washington** has approximately 185,000 citizens over 60 years of age. Many of them are on fixed incomes and are unable to afford the rising costs of household maintenance. Retirees of the King County Labor Council formed a program to do something about the situation. They provide skilled craftsmen to assist the low-income elderly with minor home repairs. In one year alone these retirees assisted more than 2,000 grateful older clients.

How to Get Started Volunteering

To learn about volunteer needs and opportunities, review all of the suggestions and tips in chapter 1. See Appendix B for a listing of groups which offer volunteer opportunities specifically for older persons.

What is Success?

To laugh often and much;

To win the respect of intelligent people and the affection of children;

To earn the appreciation of honest critics and endure the betrayal of false friends;

To appreciate beauty;

To find the best in others;

To leave the world a bit better, whether by a healthy child, a garden patch or a redeemed social condition;

To know even one life has breathed easier because you have lived;

This is to have succeeded.

—Ralph Waldo Emerson

—•8•—

Giving to Others
When You Have Less

Never stumble over anything behind you.

—Marge Simonds

Something that shocked me when I began interviewing volunteers at the Boulder Volunteer and Information Center was discovering that I was prejudiced. It was very subtle, but I definitely found it easier to like and accept some people more quickly than others. For me, it didn't seem to revolve around the common issues of race and color as much as age ("kids are irresponsible, old people are crotchety"); gender ("men make better board members and women are better nurturers and care-givers"); and appearance ("hippies are unclean and uncouth"). It took years of actually working with volunteers and seeing them in every conceivable helping situation for me to understand that who and what makes a good volunteer has nothing whatsoever to do with what is on the outside of a person. It has everything to do with what is on the inside. A loving heart and caring spirit can come in people of all ages, sizes, genders, and life circumstances. I believe this is one of the strongest messages of this book.

Another common myth is that there are "helpers" and "helpees" and that the line between the two is clearly drawn. One of the traps that volunteers and human service professionals need to guard against is to fulfill their own need to be needed by unintentionally keeping others dependent on them. After all, there can't be a helper if there isn't someone to be a helpee—right?

In *How Can I Help?*, the authors deal with this trap honestly:

> The more you think of yourself as a "therapist," the more pressure there is on someone to be a "patient." The more you identify as a "philanthropist," the more compelled someone feels to be a "supplicant." The more you see yourself as "helper," the more need for people to play the passive "helped." You're buying into, even juicing up, precisely what people who are suffering want to be rid of: limitations, dependency, helplessness, separateness.[1]

As one person who had been chronically ill and paralyzed for more than a decade said: "I have never, ever, met someone *who sees me as whole . . .*"

When we are healthy and things are going well for us, giving to others (at least for many people) seems an appropriate way of sharing our gratitude. If we give our *time* as a volunteer, as well as our money, then the return on our investment of giving can be far greater than we could ever imagine.

But how do we handle giving when we have *less* than we once had—less physical ability, or poor health, and all the problems these hardships entail? Is giving an option then? Can people who might need help also find ways to give help and discover the joy and fulfillment volunteering brings?

Giving—When You're Disabled

Let's examine what happens when the disabled are given a chance. Following is an excerpt from an article entitled "Perhaps It Just Made Us Stronger," by Homer Page, former Boulder City Councilman and County Commissioner, that appeared in the June 1989 *Handicapped Coloradan*:

> My wife and I recently spent a weekend in Washington, D.C., with another couple, whom we have known for a number of years. Like us, Jim and Betsy are blind. Jim is the Director of Governmental Affairs for the National Federation of the Blind, and Betsy is a clinical psychologist who has a private practice and teaches at Johns Hopkins University in Baltimore.
>
> During the course of the weekend the conversation came around to the topic of our blindness. Someone asked, "Did you ever think what your life would have been like if you had been sighted?"
>
> This was a particularly thought-provoking question. Most disabled people fantasize at one time or another about being able-bodied. Other people often press us, with sadness, about what we might have been if only we had not been disabled.
>
> Once in high school I took a standardized national test. I scored 296 out of 300 possible points—much higher than any of my sighted classmates. Yet my teacher asked with a touch of regret in her voice, "Did you ever wonder what you could have done if you were sighted?"
>
> She saw my life as holding only wasted potential. Every handicapped person must struggle with this commonly held belief. We must, however, resist the temptation to believe that it is true.

The article went on to describe how each of the four had evolved to their present positions. Page concluded with this observation:

> Each of us believes our lives are richer and more interesting than would have been the case had we been sighted. Because we are blind, certain doors have been closed to us. But other, better paths have appeared.

I have never heard of anyone more whole than these people. We all need to realize that "disability" is in the eye of the beholder. As H.T. Leslie said, "The game of life is not so much in holding a good hand as playing a poor hand well."

There are hundreds of stirring examples of the contributions handicapped individuals are making to others in their communities. Here are just a few:

Douglas Heir of Cherry Hill, New Jersey—an attorney and quadriplegic as a result of a diving accident, serves as an advocate for the rights of the handicapped.

Donald Caster of Cocoa Beach, Florida—although handicapped by adult muscular dystrophy, tutors children in public schools and established a program for special education students.

Alice Teal of Greenwood, Missouri—a myositis ossification handicap has not kept her from volunteering to do clerical work from her home for the conservation service.

Juanita Phelps of Kalamazoo, Michigan—although crippled by arthritis, spends nearly 70 hours a week crocheting afghans, dolls, and lap robes for hospitals and nursing homes; as well as scarves, hats, and mittens for a mission that serves the homeless.

Mary Catherine Waid of Dallas, Texas—after spending 40 years in state institutions for the mentally retarded, now lives independently and serves as an advocate for the mentally retarded to mental health professionals and legislators.

Elizabeth O'Donnell of Chicago, Illinois—in spite of being visually impaired, a diabetic, and an amputee, works almost full time as a volunteer at the Illinois Visually Handicapped Institute. She teaches Braille and independent living skills; provides intensive counseling to students; and serves as a companion, friend, and model to the residents, sharing with them her own coping skills.

These remarkable people have all been recipients of a President's Volunteer Action Award or Citation for their contributions. Still other inspiring examples are:

Ray Griggs of Livermore, California—retired after a long career with the Boy Scouts of America because of a disabling accident in the early '70s. Doctors cast a gloomy prognosis about his chances of walking normally again. Not one to take confinement to a hospital bed in stride, Ray searched for something to occupy his time and initially satisfied his need by writing to a prisoner at the Ohio State Prison. This was a rewarding experience, so when he heard about the M-2 Sponsor Program (a support program for prison inmates) at his church, he volunteered to sponsor and visit an inmate. For the next 14 years he not only sponsored inmates personally, but encouraged others to join him in reaching out to a population that most people would rather forget. In his gentle and caring fashion, Ray extended his friendship to the prison inmates and in the process greatly impacted many of their lives.

Terry Fox of Canada—won international acclaim for his courage and caring for others. Although he lost both his legs to bone cancer, he ran with his metal legs across Canada to support the cause of world hunger. As Judy Tatelbaum stated in her book, *You Don't Have to Suffer*, "He took attention off himself and his serious medical situation in order to have his life make a difference for others. It has. Taking a stand is a very powerful way of newly designing our lives."

Some people find it more fulfilling to volunteer with others, where socializing and helping go hand-in-hand. This can be especially true for disabled people for whom isolation can more easily become a reality. These examples illustrate how disabled people active in group volunteering are helping others and themselves:

Kalamazoo, Michigan Voluntary Action Center's Handi-able Project—offers training and volunteer opportunities for emotionally, physically, or mentally disabled people. They place disabled students in a variety of volunteer positions, but only after they have completed a five-unit curriculum on volunteering. Some of the volunteers' projects have included producing agency newsletters, reading at the Library for the Blind, and taking care of animals at the zoo. The project coordinator observed that "persons with disabilities have the same hopes and emotions as persons without disabilities . . . and they progress or atrophy according to their environment and opportunities."[2]

The Pensacola Special Steppers, Inc., Gulf Breeze, Florida—is a square dance troupe comprised of mentally handicapped young people and adults. It provides a recreational and social outlet for its members and serves as an example to their audiences of the capabilities of the handicapped. (President's Volunteer Action Citationist, 1987.)

The disabled are a valuable source of volunteers all too frequently overlooked by many groups and religious organizations. Our society still has a long way to go in learning to see those who may need help themselves as potential helpers, highly capable of volunteering for all types of organizations. All too frequently we withhold the precious gift of giving from this valuable source of volunteers and thus perpetuate the roles of "helper" *or* "helpee." It is possible (and necessary) to be *both*. As Lyle Schaller once said: "Nobody has any business feeling helpless, hopeless, and unneeded in a world where there is so much hurt."

We all need to work to extend the wonderfully healing gift of giving to everyone.

Giving—When You're Chronically Ill

Although people with physical or mental disabilities and those with chronic illnesses endure the consequences of many of the same stereotypes and challenges, there are some differences as well. People with illnesses like cancer, multiple sclerosis, and diabetes may have recoveries, remissions, or be able to control their illnesses and have periods of almost normal health and activity. During these times reaching out to others can be extremely beneficial for the patient's mental and emotional well-being. This is powerfully illustrated in the following excerpt from an article by Albert Fay Hill:

> People intent on "having it all" and "looking out for number one" would have a hard time understanding Shirley Jenkins. Shirley wrote no best seller, cut no platinum record and left no significant estate. But she left her signature on the spirits of people. None of the hundreds who attended her funeral was resentful or jealous of her, although many may have been envious.
>
> Shirley Jenkins had found a secret and had achieved something that eludes many of us. At her funeral a millionaire industrialist, an eminent physician, a successful politician, an artist and a dowager all wept openly. A Chicano house-painter, so ill he had to be helped to his seat by his son, grieved silently. An old rancher who

had come hundreds of miles for the service wiped his eyes and blew his nose into a colored handkerchief. One woman sat apart from the others and remembered a terrible day when Shirley had saved her sanity.

Shirley had a profound impact on such people because she had spent years visiting those who, like herself, were cancer patients.

Shirley was only 29 and the mother of an eight-year-old son when she was diagnosed as having chronic granulocytic leukemia. In searching the library for information about this type of leukemia, she found that patients typically survived three to four years. Certain she would die soon, she set about putting her affairs in order, including painting every room of her home. "I didn't want anyone coming into my house after I was gone and finding it dingy!" she said.

Two years passed and to Shirley's surprise she didn't die. Indeed, her health improved—and she had a strange emotional reaction. Brought up a no-nonsense Baptist with a strong faith, she didn't, consciously at least, resent having the disease. "But," she said, "when I had everything ready I couldn't understand why God didn't go ahead and take me. I got angry at God!" At times tension in the little family was high. Shirley said, "I felt so sorry that Don Jr. had to grow up without a mother that I was spoiling him rotten. His father was trying to discipline him—and protect me."

Finally, she was so depressed she swallowed her pride and went to her pastor for help. They talked for five hours. Shirley remembered, "He turned me around to the point where I started *living* instead of *dying*. I decided to go for it, all the way." Shirley set herself the goal of seeing her son graduate from high school. And she set about undoing some of the harm she had done the child by indulging him. Soon things returned to normal in her family.

Her doctor, Dr. Paul Hamilton, Jr., noticed the change and challenged her to try something that changed her life—and those of hundreds of other people. He asked Shirley to become a volunteer with CanSurmount, a program he and Lynn Ringer (a recovered ovarian cancer patient) had started at Denver's Presbyterian Medical Center. In this program cancer patients who have recovered or are in remission provide understanding, comfort, and support to newly-diagnosed cancer patients. (This program eventually became so popular and wide-spread that it has been taken under the wing of the American Cancer Society.)

Shirley remembered, "At first it was scary. I didn't know how to act, what to say. But I usually came away feeling better about myself. Sometimes it would give me the fear, 'Hey, that's going to be me six months from now!' That would hurt. But I grew. I came to deal with the fact that I am going to die. That part doesn't hurt as bad now. The part that hurts now is that these people have become my friends. You don't want your friends to go through pain."

As a CanSurmount volunteer she soon became so effective that Dr. Hamilton asked her to speak before groups. That was more terrifying than her disease. But later she laughed, "Dr. Hamilton is a person it's very difficult to say no to." Once she spoke before a large group of doctors, and the still shy country girl was astounded at how many physicians came to ask how they should treat their cancer patients. She became so adept at public speaking that when a radio station conducted a "leukemia-thon" to raise money for research, Shirley was chosen to represent patients. When the coordinator of volunteers at Presbyterian Medical Center died, the hospital asked Shirley to take her place.

Shirley Jenkins exceeded her goal. She not only lived to see Don Jr. graduate from high school, but also attend college, marry, and become a police officer. For the 20 years after she was diagnosed and before she died, Shirley gave courage and peace to hundreds of others who suffered from this disease.

The secret Shirley Jenkins and other CanSurmount volunteers have discovered is that when we put up a wall to protect ourselves from the suffering of others, we diminish our own souls. But when we share the pain of others, we grow until we can better appreciate and more deeply enjoy the enormous beauty of life.

(Albert Fay Hill has written an inspiring book about the CanSurmount program entitled *I'm a Patient Too*.)

When I read this remarkable story, I was reminded of one of my dearest friends, Marge Simonds. When we first met 30 years ago, she was a nurse, pilot, scuba diver, wife, and mother of two little girls. What a zest for living Marge displayed in all those roles! Then she was diagnosed as having multiple sclerosis. Over the next 25 years she gradually lost the ability to move any part of her body except her head. She eventually ended up divorced and had to go on welfare. However, despite these circumstances, she was filled with life, love, joy, and a zest for living right up until her death in 1987. Her one and only fear was that someday she might not have anything to share with others. "I still have much to learn about giving," she once said. "Heartbeats and brainwaves are indicators of physical death. To me, no longer being able to give is a form of death." The last few years of her life she counseled other MS patients by using a head-operated telephone, taught sex education classes to a youth group at her church, edited a column for her church newsletter, authored an inspirational book, and brought endless joy and laughter into my life and the lives of countless others. Marge's philosophy is reflected in this excerpt from her book, *It Occurred to Me:*[3]

Happiness Happens

Happiness happens along the way
Grab it and hold it
If just for that day.
Its moments are fleeting,
And sandwiched between
Are crises, tears and things unforseen.
We need the lows to appreciate highs
Savor them both, to deny is unwise.

Marge's optimism, appreciation, and joy permeated all that she said and did. She was an inspiration to everyone around her. Her farewell, whenever a friend left after a visit, was "Make a difference!" How much more meaningful that was than "Have a nice day" or "Take care." It became the motto for her own life and her challenge to all who knew her.

These remarkable people are poignant reminders to each of us to never underestimate what people with illnesses or disabilities can do—for themselves and for others. One of the great challenges for volunteer programs is to reach out and extend the opportunity to give to this vital group. These "helpees" want to be helpers too! Our world desperately needs what they have to give.

I am only one, but still I am one; I cannot do everything, but still I can do something; I will not refuse to do the something I can do.

—*Helen Keller*

—•9•—

Impacting the Future

A different world cannot be built by indifferent people.

—Peter Marshall

I once attended a meeting of a national board on which I serve, and during a coffee break, one of the members began talking enthusiastically about a recent trip he'd taken to be with his grandchildren. He chuckled as he related the following story:

His daughter and five-year-old grandson were vacationing in another city and someone asked the little boy where he was from. Without a moment's hesitation, the child replied, "The planet earth!"

Another board member then shared that his wife is a kindergarten teacher, and at the beginning of the school year she asked if anyone knew what day it was. A little girl's hand shot up—and she said, "It's tomorrow."

What wisdom these youngsters displayed—it *is* tomorrow and we *are* all citizens of the planet earth. I wish it were as easy for adults to grasp the significance of these remarkable realities as it is for children.

Looking toward the future is an exhilarating and challenging exercise of the imagination. But it is also a necessary and serious assignment, because the decisions we make today (as persons, citizens, religious organizations, agencies, and community groups) will determine what the future will be. This is the joy and challenge of living in a democracy—*we* are the *they* that make things happen!

This is especially true for leaders in any field, including the field of volunteerism. As Joe Nevin of Apple Computer said, "Leaders are painters of the vision and architects of the journey."

However, any credible long-range planning must be firmly grounded in knowledge of the past and present— without this it becomes ivory tower dreaming with small possibility of becoming reality. The purpose of this chapter is to provide a firm foundation for future planning for volunteerism and to provide individuals with the necessary background and foresight to enable them to effect changes as volunteers.

Understanding the Past

Change is affecting every aspect of our lives: work, home, leisure, families, makeup of our populations, technology, etc. The America of the 1990s bears little resemblance to the America of the '50s, '60s, or '70s. If volunteerism did not change to reflect these new realities, it would soon be obsolete. So let's review just a few of the most significant changes.

Major Economic Revolutions

Since volunteerism is an integral part of the fabric of this society, many major trends have impacted people's helping patterns in the past few decades. Perhaps the most significant is the enormous shift in the country's economic base.

In the early 1900s, the first major change occurred when

the U.S. shifted from being an **agricultural** to an **industrial society**. Mass migrations began as people moved from farms and small towns to the cities where the new steel, auto, rubber, and garment industries beckoned with job opportunities and unheard-of salaries. The American dream changed during those decades from "a chicken in every pot" to "two cars in every garage—and hopefully a boat or RV for weekends." By 1950, more than 65 percent of Americans worked in industry.

This great migration brought millions of people to new communities and in the process, took them away from extended family, childhood friends, and personal support systems. So people began to establish new churches, service clubs, lodges, country clubs, YMCA's and YWCA's, sports associations, and arts and cultural organizations to help them have a place to belong and to be needed.

As the industrial society became more and more complex, so did the needs of people in these cities and suburbs. A major proliferation of human service agencies and service-oriented groups were formed to address the multitude of needs and to improve the quality of life in these new communities. At this time, more organized, formal volunteering began to emerge. Hospitals, schools, youth groups, health and welfare agencies, inner-city programs, environmental and consumer groups, child and wife abuse programs, and hundreds of other such organizations realized that as the population grew, needs not only increased but also became more diverse and complex. Every organization needed the help of volunteers to help them meet these increased needs. The gratifying discovery was that literally millions of people responded to the opportunity to volunteer. Even in this transitory society, people still had a deep personal need to feel useful and to be helpful to one another.

During the last 20 years of the industrial period, when human service agencies and community organizations began to grow in number and diversity, volunteer programs within these organizations became more organized and well-defined. There was also a significant movement toward upgrading the quality of training provided for the paid staff who directed volunteer activity. The vast majority of volunteer programs today have paid volunteer directors or coordinators; clearly defined and written job descriptions; and provide interviews, training, support, and recognition for their volunteers. As people's lives became more complex and busy, it also became clear that wasting volunteers' time was not acceptable. People wanted to make a difference with whatever amount of time they had available. Volunteering in the '70s and '80s became much more complicated than it had been in the agricultural era, when lending a hand was the norm.

During the last two decades, there has been another important development designed to help volunteers sort through the myriad of needs in a community and connect them with appropriate opportunities to help. There are now more than 400 Volunteer Centers (or Voluntary Action Centers) in the U.S. and many in Canada. Their primary function is to serve as a link between volunteers and community needs. This should be the first place a prospective volunteer or group goes to learn about needs and opportunities, as it can save hours of pavement pounding and numerous false starts. (See Appendix A for a current listing of Volunteer Centers in the U.S. and Canada.)

Many communities also have Retired Senior Volunteer Programs (RSVP), which serve the same function for volunteers over 60 years of age. Look in the yellow pages of your telephone directory under Social Service Organizations or ACTION.

By the 1980s we had experienced the second major economic revolution. We changed from an **industrial society** to an **information/service society**. Writers like John Naisbitt in his book *Megatrends*, and Alvin Toffler in *The Third Wave*, graphically pointed out that the entire basis of our economy had again shifted and it was as dramatic a change as when we changed from an agricultural to an industrial society. In

1989, 70 percent of U.S. workers were employed in information or service jobs (i.e. financial institutions, computer industry, research, health, medical and human services, and food and hotel industry).

There have again been human "casualties" in this period of enormous change. Many industrial giants have either gone out of business, down-sized, or merged. This has resulted in the loss of jobs for both blue- and white-collar workers. Job security, as people once knew it, seems to be a thing of the past. Once again, a revolution has created a migration of people to wherever new jobs are available, and this uprooting has resulted in loss of personal identity and stability as people leave their jobs, friends, and home communities.

The Present—Who is Volunteering?

The contrast between the makeup of the volunteer work force 20 years ago and that work force today is quite dramatic.

Twenty years ago the vast majority of volunteers were white, middle income housewives who did not work outside the home. Many of these women made volunteering their profession and were deeply involved in community and religious organizations. Some men volunteered but their involvement was limited to such things as service clubs, sports organizations, men's clubs, and church or community boards of directors. The small number of teenagers who were involved served mostly as candy stripers in hospitals or in organizations like the Red Cross. College students tended to volunteer mostly for advocacy and cause organizations, like the Vietnam War protests.

Today, the volunteer work force is almost as diverse as the population itself and it reflects all of the societal and economic changes I mentioned previously. Following are some of the traits of today's volunteers:

■ Two-thirds of today's volunteers work outside the home.

■ Almost as many men volunteer as women (47 percent of all women volunteer; 45 percent of all men volunteer).

■ Many volunteers are from two-career marriages or are single "baby boom" professionals.

■ Single parents are well-represented.

■ Corporate-sponsored volunteer programs are becoming widespread.

■ Many people volunteer technical and professional skills.

■ High school and college students are contributing thousands of hours to a variety of causes.

■ Minority, self-help, and neighborhood volunteer groups are growing rapidly in many communities.

■ More and more handicapped and home-bound people are being given the opportunity to help others.

■ Newly retired blue- and white-collar workers, as well as seniors are a rapidly growing mainstay of the volunteer work force.

Why do we have such a dramatically different profile of volunteers today? The most obvious reason is that the profile of our population itself has changed. By studying the demographics of our country (or any community), this becomes apparent. The changes in the ages and life stages of the population directly impact who is volunteering and in what ways. Let's take a quick look at four major age groups:

Teenagers—are a significantly smaller group today than

in the previous two decades (20 percent fewer). For the first time in our nation's history, there are more people over age 65 than there are teenagers. Although fewer in number, this group is contributing a great deal through school-sponsored volunteer programs and as individuals. It is vital to continue to develop more ways for these young people to learn self-affirmation and develop confidence through giving to others. It is one way to help offset the enormous problems they face, such as alcohol and other drugs, suicide, and alienation.

Baby Boomers—are those people who were born between the years 1946-1964. There are 76 million people in this age group (45 percent of the adult population). Although they have often been referred to as the "me generation," these people have volunteered by the thousands to meet the needs in their communities. However, organizations must respond to their unique realities:

- 70 percent of the women in this group work outside the home, so both men and women need evening and weekend volunteer opportunities.

- Their work lives are both busy and uncertain due to the economic trends, so they prefer short-term, project oriented volunteer assignments.

- Two-career couples prefer to volunteer as a team, and if they have children, like to involve them too.

- Many like to share their professional skills, especially when they are underemployed.

- They favor participatory decision-making, team work, good delegation skills, ethical behavior, and a sense of humor in the organizations where they volunteer.

■ This is the most well-educated generation this nation has ever produced—25 percent have college educations—so authoritative or patronizing leadership styles do not work well with them.

■ Many baby boom women are having their first babies in their thirties or early forties and if they can, stay home with them for a year or more. They will volunteer (to keep their skills sharp), but they need help with child care costs.

The Sandwich Generation—is the group born between the years 1925-1945, and is the smallest age group of all. They have been the backbone of most volunteer programs in both community and religious organizations, and often hold several volunteer jobs simultaneously. Many of them have watched their lives change dramatically the past few years as their baby boom adult children return home (some call them "baby boomerangers"). They either can't find a job, have lost one, or have had a divorce and bring their children home with them. At the same time, this sandwich group is inheriting responsibility for their aging parents, who in many cases are also moving into their homes. This means they need to reassess their level of involvement and make hard choices about where to put their limited time. They favor shared leadership opportunities, where two can share a major assignment. Early-retired men are also a part of this group. They want significant responsibility and a worthwhile challenge utilizing the management and technical skills they spent years acquiring.

The Senior Population—those over age 65, comprise the fastest growing group. There are more than 30 million people in the U.S. over age 65; 3.3 million over age 85; and 45,000 over 100. This "chronologically gifted" group is increasing by nearly 6 million every decade and will total 87 million by the year 2040.[1] These people have become a tremendous resource to volunteer programs. (There are numerous examples of what they are doing throughout this book.) They too, have some special needs to consider:

■ Reimbursement for out-of-pocket expenses connected with volunteering (especially for those on fixed incomes).

■ Transportation to and from volunteer assignments.

■ Volunteer opportunities that are short-term, to allow time for travel and to accommodate those who are "snow birds" (those who travel south for winter months).

■ A positive attitude on the part of paid staff and other volunteers toward aging, and an appreciation of the contributions older people can and do make.

Minorities—are the fifth group greatly altering the demographic profile of America. They presently make up 20 percent of the U.S. population, but it is predicted that number will increase to 40 percent by the year 2080. Between the years 1980-85:

• **The white population increased 4.1 percent**
• **The black population increased 8.2 percent**
• **The Hispanic population increased 16 percent**
• **The Asian American population increased 37.5 percent**

These populations often volunteer in their own communities (helping out, lending a hand—as in the agricultural era), but often don't call it volunteering.

Proving that volunteering is no longer the exclusive

province of white, middle class Americans, let me share excerpts from a *Washington Post* story about an event called "A Salute to Black Women Who Make It Happen," which was put on by the National Council of Negro Women, Inc. There were over 1,000 people attending the event, held at the Washington Hilton in December 1989, and Oprah Winfrey was the emcee. Her opening remarks were: "I come celebrating the journey, I come celebrating the little passage, the movement of our women people. I include everybody because I believe that it is everybody's contribution that has allowed me to stand on solid rock here tonight . . ." She then presented awards to five outstanding black volunteers:[2]

Clementine Barfield—who founded Save Our Sons and Daughters in Detroit after her two teenage sons were slain in 1986.

Ruth Poole—who serves the poor and imprisoned in Durham, North Carolina.

Myrtle Davis—for her efforts in the health care field in St. Louis, Missouri.

Charlene Johnson—who is cofounder of REACH, an organization that fights the fallout of drugs.

Marjorie Joyner—a 93-year-old woman known as the Grand Dame of Black Beauty Culture.

One of the greatest challenges for volunteer organizations in every community will be to reflect this increasing cultural and racial diversity in their volunteer and paid staffs and on their boards of directors.

Directors and coordinators of volunteer programs around the country have had to increase their management and organizational skills in order to effectively utilize this increasingly diverse volunteer work force. It is now made up of all ages and races, males and females, working and non-employed, all coming with varied time constraints and vastly different skills and abilities. This is quite different from managing the homogeneous volunteer groups of 15-20 years ago. Those organizations that still believe that volunteers are only women who do not work outside the home are in desperate trouble.

We must be willing to enter this new era of volunteerism with a healthy mix of creativity, risk-taking, and commitment to the challenge of ensuring that volunteerism is alive and well in the new century.

This is a critical task, for as sociologist Eduard Lindeman observed two decades ago:

> I wish I knew how to induce volunteers to appreciate the significant role they play in furnishing vitality to the democratic enterprise. They are to democracy what circulation of the blood is to the organism. They keep democracy alive!

Looking Toward the Future

> *Tomorrow is the most important thing in life. It comes to us at midnite very clean. It's perfect when it arrives, and puts itself in our hands and hopes we've learned something from yesterday.*
>
> —*John Wayne*

It is important to realize that these are traumatic times. The fact is that by nature, human beings resist change. As the late columnist Sydney Harris said, "We Americans are funny about change. We both love it and hate it. What we'd really like is for things to stay the same and get better!"

The critical question before us today is not, *will* change

occur? It is rather, *how* will we as a nation, as communities, and as volunteers deal with the changes that are inevitable? Even more importantly, how can we *initiate* changes that are needed to make our world a better, safer place for all of us?

Buck Rogers, a former executive of IBM, said:

> We believe in a changing world and the future cannot be predicted with certainty. That's an obvious statement—but how we deal with change and the future is not so obvious. Change can be an ally when you're alert and sensitive and have antennae reaching in all directions picking up signals around you. Of course, change will be your enemy if it catches you by surprise. You must control change, or change will control you. To the fearful, change is threatening. But to those who love the challenge and are fast on their feet, change is stimulating and exciting. Those are the people who can make a difference because they can make things happen.[3]

We have a great opportunity to help reshape and revitalize our communities as we go through this time of restructuring. It is important for each of us to determine what we want our society to be in this new era and century, and then take personal responsibility to help bring those changes about.

George Bernard Shaw said:

> Take care to get what you like or you will be forced to like what you get. Where there is no ventilation, fresh air is declared unwholesome. Where there is no religion, hypocrisy becomes good taste. Where there is no knowledge, ignorance calls itself science.

And I would add, where there is no reaching out to help one another, there is no civilization!

Forces At Work For The Future Of Volunteerism

There are two major societal realities unfolding that I believe offer sound reasons for Americans to be optimistic about our future as a nation, and for us to believe volunteerism will thrive in the new century:

1. Increased national focus on the value of volunteerism

2. The aging of America

I. Increased National Focus on the Value of Volunteerism

President Bush took a very aggressive stance on the value of volunteerism when he said, "Any definition of a successful life must include serving others." In June 1989, he launched the 1,000 Points of Light initiative and YES (Youth Engaged in Service to America) in which he personally urged corporations, unions, and youths to address pressing social problems as volunteers. These initiatives have three major aspects:

- **To claim problems as our own**
- **To identify, enlarge, and replicate what is working**
- **To discover and encourage new leaders**

He established a foundation to encourage volunteers to fight such problems as hunger, homelessness, and illiteracy, and said the "thousand points of light" means he wants to see a vast galaxy of people and institutions working together to solve problems in their own back yard. In a January 4, 1990 White House news release, President Bush stated:

> I am committed to making community service a national policy of the highest priority. Drug abuse, illiteracy, homelessness, AIDS, environmental decay and

hunger must no longer be seen as someone else's problems for someone else to solve. To be "a point of light" is to measure your own success by what you do for someone else. Community service must become part of our daily pattern of living.

President Bush has asked that every individual connect and engage in the lives of others in need on a one-to-one basis, either independently or through an agency. He has called on all businesses, educational institutions, and media to join in.

The president wants successful unknown community programs to be identified so they can be replicated (and he gives these his 1,000 Points of Light awards). He also endorses the following:

- Serv-Net—a coalition of corporations, labor unions, and organizations to donate the services of their talented people.

- Serv-Link—new technology and more Volunteer Centers to link people with opportunities to serve as volunteers.

- New awards programs to honor outstanding voluntary efforts.

In addition, a bill was introduced in Congress in July 1989, by Edward Kennedy, called the National and Community Service Act of 1989 (s. 1430). This is a multimillion-dollar plan which includes a new Youth Service Corps, expansion of ACTION programs (Retired Senior Volunteer Program, Foster Grandparents, Senior Companions, and VISTA), new programs to increase school and college volunteer activities, and national and state service boards to coordinate community volunteer activities. There are also provisions to encourage adult volunteering in schools, business-school partnerships, and integration of community service into academic curriculums.

These are exciting indications that our nation is not just concerned about encouraging volunteers for the sake of filling gaps and providing bandaids for needs. These initiatives emphasize the responsibility each of us has as citizens of a democracy to give back some of what we have received. There is also a growing concern that we pass this ethic of service on to the next generation. It is so important that our young people understand the essence of giving as a response of gratitude for living in a free society.

There is a story about President Herbert Hoover who in 1928 was chosen as the Republican candidate for president in recognition of his great service to this country. When notified, Hoover accepted the nomination, but not the tribute. He replied, "My country owes me no debt. It gave me schooling, independence of action, and opportunity for service. My whole life has taught me what America means. I am rather indebted to my country beyond any human power to repay."

Another former president, Woodrow Wilson, had this to say about volunteerism:

> Nothing but what you volunteer has the essence of life, the springs of pleasure in it. These are the things you do because you want to do them, the things your spirit has chosen for its satisfaction . . . The more you are stimulated to such action the more clearly does it appear to you that you are a sovereign spirit, put into the world, not to wear harness, but to work eagerly without it.

II. The Aging of America

Age Wave, an exciting book by Ken Dychtwald, Ph.D., presents a very positive and optimistic view of the aging of

America's population. Let me share just a few of the author's startling facts and heartwarming conclusions:

- In 1776, the average life expectancy in the U.S. was 35, and the median age was 16.

- In 1886, the average life expectancy in the U.S. was 40, and the median age was 21.

- In 1989, the average life expectancy in the U.S. was 75, and the median age was 32.

In just a little over a century, we have added 35 years to life expectancy—which in 1776, was all there was! Today, nearly 80 percent of Americans will live past the age of 65. Dychtwald states that this senior boom, together with the birth dearth and the aging of the baby boomers, has produced a demographic revolution that has no precedent in history—our young country is growing older.[4]

For many people, this appears to be a depressing and even frightening problem developing as they focus on rising health care costs, depleting Social Security, etc. They tend to see aging as a problem instead of an opportunity. Dychtwald addresses these widely-held, negative myths about aging:[5]

Myth 1: People over 65 are old
Myth 2: Most older people are in poor health
Myth 3: Older minds are not as bright as young minds
Myth 4: Older people are unproductive
Myth 5: Older people are unattractive and sexless
Myth 6: All older people are pretty much the same

He disputes every one of these myths with impressive data and examples (i.e. most older people are not ill; only 5 percent are institutionalized; only 10 percent of those over 65 show any significant loss of memory).

Because people are living longer and retiring earlier, the average working person will have 44 percent of their life to spend on activities of choice, other than paid work.

In the chapter "Wisdom in Action," Dychtwald makes these powerful statements:

> . . . for many retirees, recreation alone may not be enough to make a life . . . many older men and women wish to spend their later years learning, growing, and doing things for others. As a result, networks of lifelong education and volunteer services are blossoming throughout America . . .

> National studies have repeatedly shown that as people grow older, they have a marked tendency to become more interested in what they give to others than in what they get. Our elders are a vital national resource . . . volunteering for every manner of helping enterprise—in the community for political and social causes, for charities—is increasingly becoming a way of life for millions of older Americans.[6]

It is obvious that many of our "chronologically gifted" Americans agree with George Bernard Shaw's eloquent statement:

> I am of the opinion that my life belongs to the whole community, and as long as I live it is my privilege to do for it whatever I can. I want to be thoroughly used up when I die, for the harder I work the more I live. I rejoice in life for its own sake. Life is no brief candle to me. It is a sort of splendid torch which I've got hold of for the moment and I want to make it burn as brightly as possible before handing it on to future generations.

With these two major societal forces comes great promise for the future of volunteerism. Not only is our society becoming more aware of the value of volunteerism and citizen involvement, but as we approach the new century, we will have more and more people available and willing to help one another as volunteers.

A Call to Action

Theodore Roosevelt once said, "Far better it is to dare mighty things, to win glorious triumphs even though checkered by failure, than to rank with those poor spirits who neither enjoy nor suffer much because they live in the gray twilight that knows neither victory nor defeat."

If we are to impact our future, we must rouse the spirit and fervor of our grassroots, ordinary citizens across the country, to tackle the enemies facing us: drugs, homelessness, illiteracy, hunger, corruption. I believe that is the dream behind President Bush's 1,000 Points of Light campaign. But 1,000 will not even make a dent in the problems—we already have 80 million. What we need is the other 55 percent of the Americans not currently volunteering to join the ranks of those already making a difference as volunteers.

It is time for our citizens to rise up with determination and an optimistic spirit and declare, Our streets *will* become safe again; our children *will* have the opportunity for a drug-free childhood and quality education; our air *will* be made safe to breathe and our water *will* become safe to drink for us and future generations; our people *will* have decent, affordable housing and food to eat . . . And then get on with the task of making those dreams our reality. Wishing will not make it so—it will take the commitment, time, and energy of all of us.

Yes, you *can* make a difference!

There's an often-told story in the Far East about the Chinese grandfather who, each day of his life, rose early, climbed to the top of a nearby hill, which blocked the early-morning sunlight, picked up a small stone, walked back down the hill and dropped the pebble on the other side of a stream near his home. His son and grandson joined him in this task. "Why do we do this?" the grandson asked.

"As long as you continue to do this and teach your children and grandchildren to carry the pebbles," the grandfather promised, "we're going to move this hill." The boy persisted, "But Grandfather, you'll never see the hill moved."

The old man nodded: "Yes, but I know that someday it will be moved."

Appendix A

Volunteer Centers

Following is a list of Volunteer Centers in the United States and Canada.[1]

ALABAMA

Volunteer and Information Center of Calhoun County
407 Noble Street • P.O. Box 1122
Anniston, AL 36202 • (205) 236-8229

United Way Volunteer and Information Center
3600 8th Avenue, South, Suite 504
Birmingham, AL 35222 • (205) 251-5131

Voluntary Action Center of Morgan County
303 Cain Street N.E., Suite D • P.O. Box 986
Decatur, AL 35602 • (205) 351-2501

Volunteer Information and Referral Center
408 West Main Street • P.O Box 405
Dothan, AL 36302 • (205) 792-4792

Volunteer Action of The Eastern Shore
150 South Greeno Road, Suite P • P.O. Box 61
Fairhope, AL 36533 • (205) 928-0509

Volunteer Center of Huntsville and Madison County
1101 Washington Street
Huntsville, AL 35801 • (205)539-7797

Volunteer Mobile
2504 Dauphin Street, Suite K
Mobile, AL 36606 • (205) 479-0631

The Voluntary Action Center
2125 East South Blvd. • P.O. Box 11044
Montgomery, AL 36116-0044 • (205)284-0006

ALASKA

Volunteer Opportunities/United Way
1901 S. Bragaw, Suite 102
Anchorage, AK 99504 • (907) 272-5579

ARIZONA

The Volunteer Bureau of the Sun Cities Area, Inc.
9451 North 99th Avenue
Peoria, AZ 85345 • (602) 972-6809

Volunteer Center of Maricopa County
1515 E. Osborn
Phoenix, AZ 85014 • (602) 263-9736

Volunteer Center of Yavapai County
116 N. Summit
Prescott, AZ 86301 • (602) 778-2531

Volunteer Center
3813 East 2nd Street
Tucson, AZ 85716 • (602) 327-6207

ARKANSAS

Voluntary Action Center
P.O. Box 3257
Little Rock, AR 72203 • (501) 376-4567

CALIFORNIA

Volunteer Center of Kern County, Inc.
601 Chester Avenue • Bakersfield, CA 93301 • (805) 327-9346

Community Action Volunteers in Education
W. 2nd and Cherry Streets
Chico, CA 95929 • (916) 895-5817

Volunteer Center of Contra Costa County
1070 Concord Avenue, Suite 100
Concord, CA 94520 • (415) 246-1050

Volunteer Bureau of Fresno, Inc.
2135 Fresno Street, Suite 304
Fresno, CA 93721 • (209) 237-3101

Volunteer Center of Orange County - North
2050 Youth Way • Fullerton, CA 92635 • (714) 526-3301

Volunteer Action Center of Nevada County
10139 Joerschke Drive
Grass Valley, CA 95945 • (916) 272-5041

La Mirada Volunteer Center
12900 Bluefield Avenue
La Mirada, CA 90638 • (213) 943-0131

Lake County Community Resource Center
P.O. Box 1776 • Lakeport, CA 95453 • (707) 263-3333

Volunteer Center of Los Angeles
621 South Virgil • Los Angeles, CA 90005 • (213) 736-1311

Volunteer Center of Los Angeles
South Central Branch
8812 South Main Street
Los Angeles, CA 90003 • (213) 753-1315

Volunteer Center of Los Angeles
City Hall Branch
200 N. Spring Street, Room 100L
Los Angeles, CA 90012 • (213) 485-6984

Volunteer Center of Los Angeles
West Los Angeles Branch
11646 W. Pico Blvd.
Los Angeles, CA 90063-1429 • (213) 445-4200

Volunteer Center of Los Angeles
East/Northeast Branch
133 N. Sunol Drive
Los Angeles, CA 90063-1429 • (213) 267-1325

Volunteer Center Orange County West
15055 Adams St., Suite A
Midway City, CA 92655 • (714) 898-0043

Volunteer Center Stanislaus
2125 Wylie Drive #6 • Modesto, CA 95355 • (209) 524-1307

Monrovia Volunteer Center
119 W. Palm Avenue • Monrovia, CA 91016 • (818) 357-3797

Volunteers in Action
444 Pearl Street, A-24 • Monterey, CA 93940 • (408) 373-6177

Volunteer Center of Napa County, Inc.
1700 Second Street, Suite 308
Napa, CA 94559 • (707) 252-6222

Volunteer Center of Alameda County, Inc.
1212 Broadway, Suite 622
Oakland, CA 94612 • (415) 893-6239

Volunteer Center of San Gabriel Valley
3301 Thorndale Road
Pasadena, CA 91107 • (818) 792-6118

Volunteers Involved for Pasadena
100 N. Garfield, #328
Pasadena, CA 91103 • (818) 405-4073

Valley Volunteer Center
333 Division Street • Pleasanton, CA 94566 • (415) 462-3570

Volunteer Center of the Greater Pomona Valley, Inc.
375 Main Street, Suite 109
Pomona, CA 91766 • (714) 623-1284

Volunteer Center of Riverside
2060 University Avenue, #206
Riverside, CA 92507 • (714) 686-4402

Volunteer Center of Sacramento
331 J Street, Suite 203
Sacramento, CA 95814 • (916) 441-4357

United Way of Salinas Valley
P.O. Box 202
Salinas, CA 93902 • (408) 424-7644

United Way of San Diego County Volunteer Bureau
4699 Murphy Canyon Road • P.O. Box 23543
San Diego, CA 92123 • (619) 492-2090

Volunteer Center of San Francisco
1090 Sansome Street
San Francisco, CA 94111 • (415) 982-8999

The Volunteer Exchange of Santa Clara County
1310 S. Bascom Avenue, Suite B
San Jose, CA 95128-4502 • (408) 286-1126

Volunteer Center of San Mateo County
436 Peninsula Avenue
San Mateo, CA 94401 • (415) 342-0801

Volunteer Center of Marin County, Inc.
70 Skyview Terrace
San Rafael, CA 94903 • (415) 479-5660

Volunteer Center Orange County - Central/South
1000 E. Santa Ana Blvd., Suite 200
Santa Ana, CA 92701 • (714) 953-5757

Volunteer Center of Santa Cruz County
1110 Emeline Avenue
Santa Cruz, CA 95060 • (408) 423-0554

Volunteer Center of Sonoma County
1041 Fourth Street • Santa Rosa, CA 95404 • (707) 544-9480

Voluntary Action Center
3333 Sandy Way • P.O. Box 14524
So. Lake Tahoe, CA 95702 • (916) 541-2611

San Joaquin Volunteer Center of United Way
P.O. Box 1585 • Stockton, CA 95201 • (209) 943-0870

Volunteer Center South Bay Harbor - Long Beach Areas
1230 Cravens Avenue • Torrance, CA 90501 • (213) 212-5009

Tulare Volunteer Bureau
P.O. Box 1704 • Tulare, CA 93275 • (209) 688-0539

Volunteer Center of San Fernando Valley
14555 Hamlin Street
Van Nuys, CA 91411-1608 • (818) 908-5066

Volunteer Center of Victor Valley
15561 Seventh Street • Victorville, CA 92392 • (619) 245-8592

The Visalia Voluntary Action Center
417 N. Locust • Visalia, CA 93291 • (209) 738-3482

COLORADO

Center for Information and Volunteer Action
P.O. Box 1248 • Aspen, CO 81612 • (303) 925-7887

Volunteer Boulder County
3305 N. Broadway, Suite 1
Boulder, CO 80302 • (303) 444-4904

Volunteer Center - Mile High United Way
2505 18th Street • Denver, CO 80211-3907 • (303) 433-8383

Volunteer Resource Bureau of United Way of Weld County
1001 9th Avenue • P.O. Box 1944
Greeley, CO 80632 • (303) 353-4300

CONNECTICUT

United Way Volunteer Center of Eastern Fairfield County
75 Washington Avenue
Bridgeport, CT 06604 • (203) 334-5106

The Volunteer Bureau of Greater Danbury
337 Main Street • Danbury, CT 06810 • (203) 797-1154

Voluntary Action Center for the Capitol Region, Inc.
880 Asylum Avenue • Hartford, CT 06105 • (203) 247-2580

Voluntary Action Center of Greater New Haven, Inc.
703 Whitney Avenue
New Haven, CT 06511 • (203) 785-1997

Voluntary Action Center of Mid-Fairfield
4 Maple Street • Norwalk, CT 06850
(203) 852-0850

Voluntary Action Center of SE Connecticut
100 Broadway
Norwich, CT 06360 • (203) 887-2519

The Volunteer Center
62 Palmer's Hill Road
Stamford, CT 06902 • (203) 348-7714

DISTRICT OF COLUMBIA

Volunteer Clearinghouse of D.C.
1313 New York Avenue, NW #303
Washington, DC 20005 • (202) 638-2664

FLORIDA

Volunteer Services of Manatee County
222 10th Street, West • Bradenton, FL 34205 • (813) 748-3411

The Volunteer Center of Volusia/Flagler Counties
444 N. Beach Street • P.O. Box 1306
Daytona Beach, FL 32015 • (904) 253-0563

Volunteer Broward
1300 South Andrews Avenue • P.O. Box 22877
Fort Lauderdale, FL 33335 • (305) 522-6761

Voluntary Action Center
2243C McGregor Blvd. • P.O. Box 2829
Fort Meyers, FL 33902 • (813) 334-0405

The Volunteer Center of Alachua County
220 N. Main Street • P.O. Box 14561
Gainesville, FL 32602 • (904) 378-2552

Volunteer Jacksonville, Inc.
1600 Prudential Drive
Jacksonville, FL 32207 • (904) 398-7777

Volunteer Center of Collier County
4050 Gulfshore Blvd., North
Naples, FL 33940 • (813) 649-4747

Volunteer Service Bureau
520 S.E. Fort King, Suite C-1
Ocala, FL 32671 • (904) 732-4771

Volunteer Center of Central Florida
1900 N. Mills Avenue, Suite 1
Orlando, FL 32803 • (407) 896-0945

Volunteer Pensacola
Voluntary Action Center, Inc.
7 North Coyle Street
Pensacola, FL 32501 • (904) 438-5649

Volunteer Center of Sarasota
2831 Ringling Blvd., #211-D
Sarasota, FL 33577 • (813) 366-0013

Voluntary Action Center
of Alternative Human Services, Inc.
5200 16th Street, N. • P.O. Box 13087
St. Petersburg, FL 33703 • (813) 527-7300

United Way Volunteer Center
851 Johnson Avenue • P.O. Box 362
Stuart, FL 34995 • (407) 220-1717

Volunteer Tallahassee, Inc.
307 East Seventh Avenue
Tallahassee, FL 32303-5520 • (904) 222-6263

Volunteer Center of Hillsboro County
4023 N. Armenia Street, Suite 300
Tampa, FL 33607 • (813) 878-2500

Volunteer Center South
101 W. Venice Avenue, Suite 25
Venice, FL 34285 • (813) 484-4305

Volunteer Center
of Palm Beach County
1639 Forum Place, Suite 3
West Palm Beach, FL 33401 • (407) 686-0080

GEORGIA

Voluntary Action Center of United Way
500 N. Slappey Blvd. • P.O. Box 3609
Albany, GA 31706 • (912) 883-6700

Volunteer Resource Center
P.O. Box 2692 • Atlanta, GA 30371 • (404) 527-7346

Help Line
630 Ellis Street • Augusta, GA 30902 • (404) 826-4484

Voluntary Action Center - Hand-up, Inc.
206 Pine Street, S.W. • P.O. Box 631
Calhoun, GA 30701 • (404) 629-7283

The Volunteer Center
1425 3rd Avenue • P.O. Box 1157
Columbus, GA 31902 • (404) 591-8657

Voluntary Action Center of NW Georgia
305 S. Thornton Avenue, Suite 2
Dalton, GA 30720 • (404) 226-4357

Volunteer Gainesville
430 Pryor Street SE • Gainesville, FL 30501 • (404) 535-5445

Volunteer Macon
2484 Ingleside Avenue A103
Macon, GA 31204 • (912) 742-6677

Voluntary Action Center of United Way
428 Bull Street • P.O. Box 9119
Savannah, GA 31401 • (912) 234-1636

Volunteer Thomasville
144 E. Jackson Street • P.O. Box 1540
Thomasville, GA 31799 • (912) 228-7673

HAWAII

Voluntary Action Center of Oahu
200 N. Vineyard Blvd., Room 603
Honolulu, HI 96817 • (808) 536-7234

IDAHO

Lewis-Clark Volunteer Bureau
413 Main - Room 210 • Lewiston, ID 83501 • (208) 746-0136

ILLINOIS

The Volunteer Center of NW Suburban Chicago
306 W. Park Street
Arlington Heights, IL 60005 • (312) 398-1320

Volunteer Center - United Way/Crusade of Mercy
125 S. Clark Street • Chicago, IL 60603-4012 • (312) 580-2723

Volunteer Center of the Greater Quad Cities
1417 6th Avenue • Moline, IL 61265 • (309) 764-6804

United Way Volunteer Center
1802 Woodfield Drive • Box 44
Savoy, IL 61874 • (217) 352-5151

Community Volunteer Center
Lincoln Land Community College • Shepherd Road
Springfield, IL 62794-9256 • (217) 786-2430

Voluntary Action Center of Dekalb County
1606 Bethany Road • Sycamore, IL 60178 • (815) 758-0818

DuPage County Human Services
Volunteer Development Unit
421 N. County Farm Road
Wheaton, IL 60187 • (312) 682-7586

INDIANA

First Call for Help/Volunteer Services
646 Franklin • P.O. Box 827
Columbus, IN 47202 • (812) 376-0011

Volunteer Action Center
101 NW First Street
Old Post Office Place • P.O. Box 18
Evansville, IN 47701 • (812) 464-8585

Volunteer Connection
227 East Washington Blvd., Suite 204
Fort Wayne, IN 46802 • (219) 420-4263

The Window Community Volunteer Center
223 S. Main Street
Goshen, IN 46526 • (219) 533-9680

Voluntary Action Center of the Lake Area
221 West Ridge Road
Griffith, IN 46319 • (219) 923-2302

Volunteer Action Center
1828 N. Meridian Street
Indianapolis, IN 46202 • (317) 923-1466

Volunteers in Community Service of Howard County, Inc.
105 W. Sycamore Street, Suite 200
Kokomo, IN 46901 • (317) 457-4481

Community Resource Center of St. Joseph County, Inc.
914 Lincolnway West
South Bend, IN 46601 • (219) 232-2522

Volunteer Action Center
721 Wabash Avenue, Suite 502
Terre Haute, IN 47807 • (812) 232-8822

IOWA

Volunteer Bureau of Story County
510 5th Street
Ames, IA 50010 • (505) 232-2736

Volunteer Bureau of Council Bluffs
722 Creek Top
Council Bluffs, IA 51503 • (712) 323-1673

Volunteer Center of United Way of Central Iowa
1111 Ninth Street, Suite 300
Des Moines, IA 50314 • (515) 246-6545

The Voluntary Action Center of Muscatine
501 Sunset Drive
Muscatine, IA 52761 • (319) 263-0959

VAC of the Iowa Great Lakes, Inc.
1713 Hill Avenue
Spirit Lake, IA 51360 • (712) 336-4444

KANSAS

Volunteer Center of Wyandotte County
710 Minnesota Avenue • P.O. Box 17-1042
Kansas City, KS 66117 • (913) 371-3674

Volunteer Center of Johnson County
5311 Johnson Drive • Mission, KS 66205 • (913) 432-0766

Volunteer Center of Topeka, Inc.
4125 Gage Center Drive, Suite 214
Topeka, KS 66604 • (913) 272-8890

United Way Volunteer Center
212 N. Market Street, Suite 200
Wichita, KS 67202 • (316) 267-1321

KENTUCKY

Volunteer Center of Frankfort/Franklin County, Inc.
401 West Main Street • P.O. Box 183
Frankfort, KY 40602 • (502) 227-7702

Volunteer Center of the Bluegrass
2029 Bellefonte Drive • Lexington, KY 40503 • (606) 278-6258

United Way Voluntary Action Center
334 East Broadway • P.O. Box 4488
Louisville, KY 40204-0488 • (502) 583-2821

The Volunteer Center
920 Frederica Street, Suite 404 • P.O. Box 123
Owensboro, KY 42302 • (502) 683-9161

LOUISIANA

Volunteer Baton Rouge
8776 Bluebonnet Blvd.
Baton Rouge, LA 70810 • (504) 767-1698

Volunteer Center of Lafayette
1120 Coolidge, Complex I
Lafayette, LA 70503 • (318) 233-1006

Volunteer Center of SW Louisiana
125 W. Jefferson Drive
Lake Charles, LA 70605 • (318) 477-8483

United Way Volunteer Center
1300 Hudson Lane, Suite 7
Monroe, LA 71201 • (318) 325-3869

Volunteer And Information Agency, Inc.
4747 Earhart Blvd., Suite 111
New Orleans, LA 70125 • (504) 488-4636

MAINE

United Way of York County
4 Dane Street • P.O. Box 727
Kennebunk, ME 04043-07 • (207) 985-3359

The Center for Voluntary Action of Greater Portland
233 Oxford Street • Portland, ME 04101 • (207) 874-1015

MARYLAND

Volunteer Center of Frederick County
22 S. Market Street • Frederick, MD 21701 • (301) 663-0011

Anne Arundel County/Community Services
Anne Arundel Center North • 101 Crain Highway, Suite 505
Glen Burnie, MD 21061 • (301) 787-6880

Prince Georges Voluntary Action Center, Inc.
6309 Baltimore Avenue, Suite 305
Riverdale, MD 20737 • (301) 779-9444

Volunteer Center
50 Monroe Street, #400
Rockville, MD 20850 • (301) 217-9100

MASSACHUSETTS

VAC United Way of Massachusetts Bay
2 Liberty Square • Boston, MA 02109 • (617) 482-8370

Volunteer Service Bureau of Taunton
P.O. Box 416 • Taunton, MA 02780 • (508) 824-3985

Volunteer Resources Division
United Way of Central Massachusetts
484 Main Street, Suite 300
Worcester, MA 01608 • (617) 757-5631

MICHIGAN

Voluntary Action Center
2301 Platt Road • Ann Arbor, MI 48104 • (313) 971-5852

Volunteer Bureau of Battle Creek
182 W. Van Buren Street
Battle Creek, MI 49017 • (616) 965-0555

Volunteer Action Center
1308 Columbus Avenue • Bay City, MI 48708 • (517) 893-6060

The Center for Volunteer/
United Community Services of Metro Detroit
1212 Greswold at State
Detroit, MI 48226-1899 • (313) 226-9429

Voluntary Action Center, Information and Referral Service
202 E. Boulevard Drive, Room 110
Flint, MI 48503 • (313) 767-0500

Volunteer Center/United Way of Kent County
500 Commerce Building
Grand Rapids, MI 49503 • (616) 459-6281

VAC of Greater Kalamazoo
709-A Westnedge Street
Kalamazoo, MI 49007 • (616) 382-8350

Voluntary Action Center
300 N. Washington Square, Suite 202
Lansing, MI 48933 • (517) 371-4894

Voluntary Action Center of Midland County, Inc.
1714 Eastman Road • Midland, MI 48640 • (517) 631-7660

Southwestern Michigan Volunteer Center
1213 Oak Street • Niles, MI 49120 • (616) 683-5464

Voluntary Action Center of Saginaw County
118 E. Genesee • Saginaw, MI 48607 • (517) 755-2822

MINNESOTA

Voluntary Action Center
402 Ordean Building, 424 W. Superior Street
Duluth, MN 55802 • (218) 726-4776

United Way's Voluntary Action Center
404 South 8th Street
Minneapolis, MN 55404 • (612) 340-7532

The Volunteer Connection, Inc.
903 W. Center, Suite 200
Rochester, MN 55902 • (507) 287-2244

United Way's Voluntary Action Center
26 N. 6th Avenue, Suite 20 • P.O. Box 698
St. Cloud, MN 56302 • (612) 252-0227

Voluntary Action Center of the St. Paul Area
251 Starkey Street, Suite 127 • Bolander Building
St. Paul, MN 55107 • (612) 227-3938

Community Volunteer Service of the St. Croix Valley Area
115 S. Union Street
Stillwater, MN 55082 • (612) 439-7434

MISSISSIPPI

Volunteer Center of United Way
P.O. Drawer 23169
Jackson, MS 39225-3169 • (601) 354-1765

Volunteer Jackson County
3510 Magnolia Street • P.O. Box 97
Pascagoula, MS 39567 • (601) 762-8557

MISSOURI

Voluntary Action Center
111 South Ninth • 200 Strollway Centre
Columbia, MO 65201 • (314) 449-6959

Voluntary Action Center Eastern Jackson County
10901 Winner Road, Suite 211
Independence, MO 64052 • (816) 252-2636

Volunteer Center
Heart of America United Way
605 West 47th Street, Suite 300
Kansas City, MO 64112 • (816) 531-1945

Voluntary Action Center
401 N. 12th Street • P.O. Box 188
St. Joseph, MO 64502-0188 • (816) 364-2381

United Way of Greater St. Louis VAC
1111 Olive
St. Louis, MO 63101 • (314) 421-0700

MONTANA

Community Help Line
113 6th Street N.
Great Falls, MT 59401 • (406) 761-6010

NEBRASKA

United Way Volunteer Bureau
1805 Harney St.
Omaha, NE 68102 • (402) 342-8232

Scotts Bluff County Volunteer Bureau
1721 Broadway, Room 409
Scottsbluff, NE 69361 • (308) 632-3736

NEVADA

United Way Volunteer Bureau
1055 E. Tropicana, #300
Las Vegas, NV 89119 • (702) 798-4636

VAC/United Way of No. Nevada
500 Ryland Street • P.O. Box 2730
Reno, NV 89505-2730 • (702) 322-8668

NEW HAMPSHIRE

Monadnock Volunteer Center
331 Main Street • Keene, NH 03431 • (603) 352-2088

Voluntary Action Center
102 N. Main Street • Manchester, NH 03102 • (603) 668-8601

NEW JERSEY

The Volunteer Center of Atlantic City
1125 Atlantic Avenue, 4th Floor
Atlantic City, NJ 08401 • (609) 344-7011

Volunteer Bureau of Bergen County
64 Passaic Street
Hackensack, NJ 07601 • (201) 489-9454

VAC of Delaware Valley United Way
3131 Princeton Pike, Bldg. #4
Lawrenceville, NJ 08648 • (609) 896-1912

Voluntary Action Center of Morris County
36 South Street • Morristown, NJ 07960 • (201) 538-7200

Voluntary Action Center of Middlesex County
100 Livingston Avenue
New Brunswick, NJ 08901 • (201) 249-8910

Volunteer Center of Greater Essex County, Inc.
303-309 Washington Street, 5th Floor
Newark, NJ 07102 • (201) 622-3737

Volunteer Center of Monmouth County
188 East Bergen Place • Red Bank, NJ 07701 • (201) 741-3330

Volunteer Center for Somerset County
205 W. Main Street, 4th Floor • P.O. Box 308
Somerville, NJ 08876-0308 • (201) 725-6640

NEW MEXICO

The Volunteer Center of Albuquerque
302 Eighth Street, NW •P.O. Box 1767
Albuquerque, NM 87103 • (505) 247-3671

Volunteer Involvement Service
LaSalle B-108 • College of Santa Fe
Santa Fe, NM 87501 • (505) 473-1000

NEW YORK

The Volunteer Center of Albany, Inc.
340 First Street • Albany, NY 12206 • (518) 434-2061

Voluntary Action Center
Vestal Parkway E. at Jensen Road • P.O. Box 550
Binghamton, NY 13902 • (607) 729-2592

**Volunteer Center of the United Way
of Buffalo/Erie Counties**
742 Delaware Avenue
Buffalo, NY 14209 • (716) 887-2692

**Volunteer Connection of United Way
of SE Steuben County**
22 W. 3rd Street • Corning, NY 14830 • (607) 962-4644

Nassau County Voluntary Action Center
320 Old Country Road
Garden City, NY 11530 • (516) 535-3897

Voluntary Action Center, Inc.
65 Ridge Street • Glens Falls, NY 12801 • (518) 793-3817

VAC of Suffolk County
90 High Street • Huntington, NY 11743 • (516) 549-1867

Volunteer Service Bureau
c/o United Way of S. Chautauqua County
101 East 4th St. • P.O. Box 1012
Jamestown, NY 14702-1012 • (716) 483-1561

Mayor's Voluntary Action Center
61 Chambers Street • New York, NY 10007 • (212) 566-5950

United Way of Greater Rochester, Inc.
55 St. Paul Street • Rochester, NY 14604 • (716) 454-2770

Rome Voluntary Action Center
City Hall on the Mall • Rome, NY 13440 • (315) 336-5638

Volunteer Center of the Human Services Planning Council
152 Barrett Street • Schenectady, NY 12305 • (518) 372-3395

Volunteer Center, Inc.
115 E. Jefferson Street, Suite 300
Syracuse, NY 13202 • (315) 474-7011

Volunteer Bureau of the Mohawk-Hudson Area
502 Broadway • P.O. Box 156
Troy, NY 12181 • (518) 274-7234

Voluntary Action Center of Greater Utica, Inc.
1644 Genesee Street
Utica, NY 13502 • (315) 735-4463

Volunteer Service Bureau of Westchester
470 Mamaroneck Avenue
White Plains, NY 10605 • (914) 948-4452

NORTH CAROLINA

Volunteer Service Bureau
50 S. French Broad Avenue
Asheville, NC 28801 • (704) 255-0696

Brunswick County Volunteer and Information Center, Inc.
County Courthouse, Room 110 • P.O. Box 71
Bolivia, NC 28422 • (919) 253-4441

United Way/Voluntary Action Center
301 South Brevard Street
Charlotte, NC 28202 • (704) 372-7170

Volunteer Center of Greater Durham, Inc.
119 Orange Street • Durham, NC 27701 • (919) 688-8977

Voluntary Action Center of Greensboro, Inc.
1301 N. Elm Street • Greensboro, NC 27401 • (919) 373-1633

Volunteer Center of Vance County, Inc.
414 S. Garnett Street • P.O. Box 334
Henderson, NC 27536 • (919) 492-1540

Volunteer Service Bureau
475 South Church Street • P.O. Box 487
Hendersonville, NC 28793 • (704) 692-8700

Volunteer Center of Greater High Point
Holt McPherson Center • 305 N. Main Street
High Point, NC 27260 • (919) 883-4127

United Way of Wake County Voluntary Action Center
1100 Wake Forest Road • Raleigh, NC 27604 • (919) 833-5739

Volunteer Center - United Way
311 W. 4th Street
Winston-Salem, NC 27101 • (919) 723-3601

NORTH DAKOTA

Missouri Slope Areawide United Way
P.O. Box 2111 • Bismarck, ND 58502 • (701) 255-3601

United Way's Volunteer Center
315 N. Eighth Street • P.O. Box 1609
Fargo, ND 58107-1609 • (701) 237-5050

United Way/Community Services
323 1/2 De Mers Avenue • P.O. Box 207
Grand Forks, ND 58206-0207 • (701) 775-0671

OHIO

The Volunteer Center
500 West Exchange Street
Akron, OH 44302 • (216) 762-8991

Voluntary Action Center/A Service of United Way
618 Second Street, NW • Canton, OH 44703 • (216) 453-9172

Info-Line/Volunteer Bureau
10823 Mayfield Road • Chardon, OH 44024 • (216) 729-7931

VAC/United Appeal and Community Chest
2400 Reading Road • Cincinnati, OH 45202 • (513) 762-7171

The Volunteer Center, United Way Services
3100 Euclid Avenue • Cleveland, OH 44115 • (216) 361-1010

CALLVAC
370 South Fifth Street
Columbus, OH 43215 • (614) 221-6766

Voluntary Action Center of United Way
184 Salem Avenue • Dayton, OH 45406 • (513) 225-3066

United Way of Hamilton, Fairfield, Ohio and Vicinity, Inc.
323 North Third Street
Hamilton, OH 45011 • (513) 844-1705

United Way Voluntary Action Center
570 N. St. Rt. 741 • Lebanon, OH 45036 • (513) 933-2248

Volunteer Lima
c/o Churchpeople for Change and Reconciliation
221 West North Street • Lima, OH 45801 • (419) 229-6949

Medina County Organization on Volunteering
246 Northland Drive
Medina, OH 44256 • (216) 723-9614

Voluntary Action Center of Erie County, Inc.
158 E. Market Street, Room 610
Sandusky, OH 44870 • (419) 627-0074

Volunteer Service Bureau
616 N. Limestone Street
Springfield, OH 45503 • (513) 322-4262

Voluntary Action Center
1 Stranahan Square, Suite 141
Toledo, OH 43604 • (419) 244-3063

CONTACT Community Connection
P.O. Box 1403
Warren, OH 44482-1403 • (216) 395-5255

The Volunteer Registry
Wayne/Holmes Information and Referral Exchange
4431 N. Market Street
Wooster, OH 44691 • (216) 264-9473

OKLAHOMA

Volunteer Center
1430 S. Boulder • Tulsa, OK 74119 • (918) 585-5551

OREGON

Voluntary Action Center/YMCA
2055 Patterson • Eugene, OR 97405 • (503) 686-9622

Volunteer Bureau of Greater Portland
718 West Burnside, Room 404
Portland, OR 97209 • (503) 222-1355

PENNSYLVANIA

Voluntary Action Center of the Lehigh Valley
520 E. Broad Street • Bethlehem, PA 18018 • (215) 691-6670

The Franklin County Volunteer Center, Inc.
170 Mill Road • Chambersburg, PA 17201 • (717) 261-1133

Volunteer Center of Clearfield County
c/o Clearfield County Area Agency on Aging
103 N. Frost Street • Clearfield, PA 16830 • (814) 765-2696

COVE/Council on Volunteers for Erie County
110 West 10th Street • Erie, PA 16501-1466 • (814) 456-2937

Tri-County Volunteer Action Center
122 Chestnut Street • Harrisburg, PA 17101 • (717) 238-6678

Lancaster Volunteer Service Center
630 Janet Avenue • Lancaster, PA 17601 • (717) 299-2821

Volunteer Action Council, Inc.
Seven Benjamin Franklin Parkway
Philadelphia, PA 19103 • (215) 568-6360

Volunteer Action Center
United Way of Allegheny County
200 Ross Street • P.O. Box 735
Pittsburgh, PA 15230 • (412) 261-6010

Voluntary Action Center of NE Pennsylvania
225 N. Washington Avenue
Scranton, PA 18503 • (717) 347-5616

Voluntary Action Center of Centre County, Inc.
1524 W. College Avenue, #8
State College, PA 16801-2715 • (814) 234-8222

**The Clyde J. Tracanna Volunteer Resource Center
of Washington County**
c/o United Way of Washington County
58 East Cherry Avenue
Washington, PA 15301 • (412) 225-3310

Volunteer Action Center
United Way of Wyoming Valley
9 E. Market Street
Wilkes-Barre, PA 18711-0351 • (717) 822-3020

The Volunteer Center of York County
800 E. King St.-United Way Bldg.
York, PA 17403 • (717) 846-4477

RHODE ISLAND

Volunteers in Action, Inc.
229 Waterman Street • Providence, RI 02906 • (401) 421-6547

SOUTH CAROLINA

Volunteer and Information Center of Beaufort
706 Bay Street • P.O. Box 202
Beaufort, SC 29901-0202 • (803) 524-4357

VAC-Trident United Way
1069 King Street • P.O. Box 2696
Charleston, SC 29403 • (803) 723-1676

United Way Voluntary Action Center
1800 Main Street • P.O. Box 152
Columbia, SC 29202 • (803) 733-5400

Volunteer Greenville - A Volunteer Center
301 University Ridge, Suite 5300
Greenville, SC 29601-3672 • (803) 232-6444

Voluntary Action Center
Box 4759 • Hilton Head Island, SC 29938 • (803) 785-6646

United Way of the Piedmont, Volunteer Center
101 East St. John Street, Suite 307 • P.O. Box 5624
Spartanburg, SC 29304 • (803) 582-7556

Volunteer Sumter, Inc.
34 E. Calhoun • P.O. Box 957
Sumter, SC 29150 • (803) 775-9424

SOUTH DAKOTA

Volunteer and Information Center
304 S. Phillips, Suite 310
Sioux Falls, SD 57102 • (605) 339-4357

TENNESSEE

Voluntary Action Center
451 River Street • P.O. Box 4029
Chattanooga, TN 37405 • (615) 265-0514

Volunteer - Johnson City, Inc.
200 E. Main Street, Suite 202 • P.O. Box 1443
Johnson City, TN 37605 • (615) 926-8010

Volunteer - East Tennessee State University
Student Activities Center • P.O. Box 21040A
Johnson City, TN 37614 • (615) 929-5675

Volunteer Kingsport
1701 Virginia Avenue • Kingsport, TN 37664 • (615) 247-4511

Volunteer Center of United Way of Greater Knoxville, Inc.
1514 East Fifth Avenue • P.O. Box 326
Knoxville, TN 37901-0326 • (615) 523-9135

Volunteer Center of Memphis
263 S. McLean Blvd. • Memphis, TN 38104 • (901) 276-8655

Volunteer Center - United Way of Nashville
250 Venture Circle • P.O. Box 24667
Nashville, TN 37202 • (615) 255-8501

TEXAS

Volunteer Center of Abilene, Inc.
First National Bank Tower, Suite 880 • P.O. Box 3953
Abilene, TX 79604 • (915) 677-8954

Volunteer Action Center of the United Way
2207 Line Avenue • P.O. Box 3069
Amarillo, TX 79116-3069 • (806) 376-6714

Volunteer Resource Center of Brazoria County
P.O. Drawer 909 • Angleton, TX 77516 • (409) 849-4404

Volunteer Center of the Coastal Bend
1721 S. Brownlee Blvd.
Corpus Christi, TX 78404 • (512) 887-4545

Volunteer Center of Dallas County
2816 Swiss
Dallas, TX 75204 • (214) 744-1194

Volunteer Bureau of United Way
1918 Texas Street • P.O. Box 3488
El Paso, TX 79923 • (915) 532-4919

Volunteer Center of Metropolitan Tarrant County
210 E. 9th Street • Fort Worth, TX 76102-6494 • (817) 878-0099

Volunteers in Service to Others
P.O. Box 607 • Gainesville, TX 76240 • (817) 668-6403

The Volunteer Center of the Texas Gulf Coast
3100 Timmons Lane, Suite 100
Houston, TX 77027 • (713) 965-0031

The Volunteer Center of Longview
1109 N. 4th Street • P.O. 3443
Longview, TX 75606 • (214) 758-2374

Volunteer Resource Center
P.O. Box 3415 • McAllen, TX 78502 • (512) 781-2191

The Volunteer Center of Midland
1030 Andrews Highway, Suite 207 • P.O. Box 2145
Midland, TX 79702 • (915) 697-8781

Volunteer Center of Plano
301 W. Parker Road, Suite 213
Plano, TX 75023 • (214) 422-1050

United Way Volunteer Center
P.O. Box 898 • San Antonio, TX 78293-0898 • (512) 224-5000

Volunteer Services Bureau
3000 Texas Blvd. • Texarkana, TX 75503 • (214) 793-4903

The Volunteer Center
201 West Waco Drive • P.O. Box 2027
Waco, TX 76703 • (817) 753-5683

UTAH

Voluntary Action Center
240 N. 100 East • P.O. Box 567
Logan, UT 84321 • (801) 752-3103

Weber County Volunteer Center
2650 Lincoln, Rm. 268 • Ogden, UT 84401 • (801) 625-3777

United Way Community Services, Inc.
60 E. 100 S. • P.O. Box 135 • Provo, UT 84603 • (801) 374-8108

Voluntary Action Center of Community Services Council
212 W. 1300 South • Salt Lake City, UT 84115 • (801) 486-2136

VIRGINIA

Alexandria Volunteer Bureau
801 N. Pitt Street, Suite 102
Alexandria, VA 22314 • (703) 836-2176

The Arlington Volunteer Office
2100 Clarendon Blvd. • #1 Courthouse Plaza, Suite 106
Arlington, VA 22201 • (703) 358-3222

Volunteer Center of Montgomery County
Corner of W. Roanoke and Otey Streets • P.O. Box 565
Blacksburg, VA 24060-0565 • (703) 552-4909

Volunteer - Bristol
P.O. Box 1599 • Bristol, VA 24203 • (703) 669-1555

United Way Volunteer Center
413 E. Market, Suite 101 • P.O. Box 139
Charlottesville, VA 22902 • (804) 972-1705

Voluntary Action Center of Fairfax County Area, Inc.
10530 Page Avenue • Fairfax, VA 22030 • (703) 246-3460

Voluntary Action Center of the Virginia Peninsula
1520 Aberdeen Road, Suite 109
Hampton, VA 23666 • (804) 838-9770

Voluntary Action Center of Central Virginia
1010 Miller Park Square • P.O. Box 2434
Lynchburg, VA 24501 • (804) 847-8657

Voluntary Action Center of the Prince William Area
9300 Peabody Street, Suite 104
Manassas, VA 22110 • (703) 369-5292

Volunteer Action Center of S. Hampton Roads
253 W. Freemason St. • Norfolk, VA 23510 • (804) 624-2403

Volunteer Action Center of Southwest Virginia
Route 19, SVCC Training Center • P.O. Box SVCC
Richlands, VA 24641 • (703) 964-4218

Volunteer Center of United Way of Greater Richmond
4001 Fitzhugh Avenue • P.O. Box 6649
Richmond, VA 23230-0049 • (804) 353-2000

Voluntary Action Center
920 South Jefferson Street • P.O. Box 496
Roanoke, VA 24003 • (703) 985-0131

WASHINGTON

Volunteer Center of Whatcom County
2111 King Street • Bellingham, WA 98225 • (206) 733-3290

United Way Volunteer Center of Lewis County
500 N. Pearl • Box 5 • Centralia, WA 98531 • (206) 330-2122

United Way of Snohomish County - Volunteer Center
4526 Federal • P.O. Box 2977
Everett, WA 98203-0977 • (206) 258-4521

Volunteer Center Benton/Franklin Counties
205 N. Dennis • Kennewick, WA 99336 • (509) 783-0631

Voluntary Action Center/SCCAA
613 South Second • P.O. Box 1507
Mt. Vernon, WA 98273 • (206) 336-6627

United Way Volunteer Center of King County
107 Cherry Street • Seattle, WA 98104 • (206) 461-3751

United Way's Volunteer Center
P.O. Box 326 • Spokane, WA 99210-0326 • (509) 838-6581

Volunteer Center of United Way of Pierce County
734 Broadway • P.O. Box 2215
Tacoma, WA 98401 • (206) 272-4267

Volunteer Bureau of Clark County
1703 Main Street • P.O. Box 425
Vancouver, WA 98660-2607 • (206) 694-6577

Greater Yakima Volunteer Bureau
302 W. Lincoln • Yakima, WA 98902 • (509) 248-4460

WISCONSIN

United Way Volunteer Bureau
120 N. Morrison Street • P.O. Box 1091
Appleton, WI 54912 • (414) 739-5126

Volunteer Service Bureau/VAC
431 Olympian Blvd. • Beloit, WI 53511 • (608) 365-1278

Volunteer Center
338 S. Chestnut • Green Bay, WI 54303 • (414) 435-1101

Kenosha Voluntary Action Center
716 58th Street • Kenosha, WI 53140 • (414) 654-4554

Voluntary Action Center/United Way of Dane County
2059 Atwood Avenue • Madison, WI 53704 • (608) 246-4380

Volunteer Center of Greater Milwaukee, Inc.
600 E. Mason Street • Milwaukee, WI 53202 • (414) 273-7887

Voluntary Action Center of Waukesha County, Inc.
2220 Silvernail Road • Pewaukee, WI 53072 • (414) 544-0150

The United Way Volunteer Center
1045 Clark Street, #204
Stevens Point, WI 54481 • (715) 341-6740

Wausau Area Volunteer Exchange
407 Grant Street • Wausau, WI 54401 • (715) 845-5279

Volunteer Center of Washington County
120 N. Main Street, Suite 340
West Bend, WI 53095 • (414) 338-8256

WYOMING

Volunteer Information Center
406 E. 17th Street • P.O. Box 404
Cheyenne, WY 82003 • (307) 632-4132

CANADA

The Volunteer Bureau of Fredericton United Way
P.O. Box 164
Fredericton, NB, Canada E3B 4Y9 • (506) 459-7772

Central Volunteer Bureau
415 Dundas Street
London, ONT, Canada N6B 1V9 • (519) 438-4155

Volunteer Centre Du Benevolat
Suite No. 406, 236 St. George Street
Moncton, NB, Canada E1C 1W1 • (506) 857-8005

Saint John Volunteer Centre, Inc.
P.O. Box 7091, Sta. A
Saint John, NB Canada E21 4S5 • (506) 658-1555

Volunteer Ontario
111 Merton Street, Suite 207
Toronto, ONT, Canada M4S 3A7 • (416) 487-6139

Volunteer Vancouver
3102 Main Street • Suite 301
Vancouver, BC, Canada V5T 3G7 • (604) 875-9144

Appendix B

Volunteer Organizations for Seniors

The excellent book, *Beyond Success*, lists the following organizations as having volunteer opportunities specifically for older people.[1]

American Association of Retired Persons
1909 K Street, N.W.
Washington, DC 20049 • (202) 872-4700

More than 28 million people aged fifty and over are members of the American Association of Retired Persons (AARP). Members are active in community, state, and national affairs. Through approximately 3,500 AARP chapters and 2,600 Retired Teachers Association units across the country, members can become involved in volunteer service and fellowship activities. To assist local groups, AARP maintains a volunteer network of more than 6,000 officials in 10 geographic regions. An additional 30,000 volunteers serve in such programs as Tax-Aide, Medicare assistance, and driver improvement. Others participate in state and local legislative activities. AARP's Volunteer Talent Bank gives interested members and other older people access to AARP volunteer opportunities as well as positions in other volunteer organizations. To register, contact AARP.

Foster Grandparent Program • ACTION
806 Connecticut Avenue, N.W., Room 1006
Washington, DC 20525 • (202) 634-9349 and (800) 424-8867

Through the Foster Grandparent Program (FGP)—run by ACTION, the federal domestic volunteer agency—low-income Americans aged sixty and older provide person-to-person service to children. In 1986, through 249 FGP projects, some 19,000 volunteers gave close to 20 million hours to children suffering from various disabilities—abuse and neglect, handicaps, drug and alcohol abuse, mental retardation, illiteracy, and delinquency. Foster grandparents serve four hours a day, five days a week, through nonprofit agencies such as schools, hospitals, juvenile detention centers, Head Start, shelters, state schools, and drug rehabilitation centers. The program allows volunteers a stipend of $2.50 per hour, transportation and meal assistance, and insurance.

Gray Panthers
311 South Juniper Street, Suite 601
Philadelphia, Pennsylvania 19107 • (215) 545-6555

The Gray Panthers, founded in 1970, seek to promote an intergenerational philosophy and positive attitudes toward aging and to oppose age discrimination. The group works for the greater collective empowerment of all people, including the dependent, and encourages a greater appreciation of the racial, ethnic, and cultural diversity of American society. Specific areas of interest include Social Security, access to health care, a national health service, peace, nursing home reform, the rights of the disabled, and housing. The Gray Panthers have 70,000 national members-at-large plus an active chapter membership of about 10,000. The nearly 100 chapters in almost 30 states have a high degree of autonomy on issue emphasis and tactical decisions.

International Executive Service Corps
8 Stamford Forum • P.O. Box 10005
Stamford, Connecticut 60904-2005 • (203) 967-6000

International Executive Service Corps (IESC) recruits retired, highly skilled U.S. executives and technical advisers to share their years of experience with businesses in the developing nations. The men and women selected by IESC work as volunteers. They serve as advisers on short-term assignments, implement improvements, and develop guidelines that the client can follow in the future. IESC has answered requests to help businesses ranging from the manufacture of handbags to steel mills. Working in 84 nations, since advisers were first sent abroad in 1965, IESC has completed over 11,000 projects and has some 9,000 experienced men and women ready to supply their expertise.

National Executive Service Corps
257 Park Avenue South
New York, New York 10003 • (212) 867-5010

The National Executive Service Corps (NESC) is a management consulting organization dedicated to improving the effectiveness of organizations that exist for the betterment of society. NESC provides management improvement services that utilize the experience of retired senior-level business people. These seasoned consultants contribute their time to achieve solutions to operational problems for a broad spectrum of educational, health, social service, cultural, and religious organizations. Consulting assignments average six months and conclude with written analyses and recommendations for future action. NESC serves clients in all regions of the country and has helped organize 30 independent Executive Service Corps throughout the United States.

Older Women's League
730 11th Street, N.W., Suite 300
Washington, DC 20001 • (202) 783-6686

The Older Women's League (OWL) is a national membership organization addressing the special concerns of mid-life and older women. OWL's purpose is to propose solutions to the difficult problems women face as they age and to educate and support women as they pursue these solutions. OWL's agenda currently is focused on such issues as Social Security reform, pension rights, health care in retirement, job opportunities, and care-giver support services. OWL chapters are located in 100 communities in 35 states, with a membership of 17,000. With the exception of a small, Washington-based staff, OWL is an all-volunteer organization. Volunteers work on the board of directors, do fund-raising and other support activities, and are involved with issues advocacy.

Retired Senior Volunteer Program • ACTION
806 Connecticut Avenue, N.W., Room 1006
Washington, DC 20525 • (202) 634-9353 and (800) 424-8867

In 1986, the Retired Senior Volunteer Program (RSVP)—run by ACTION, the federal domestic volunteer agency—celebrated its fifteenth anniversary. Through 750 projects, 365,000 volunteers aged 60 or over were assigned to 51,000 community agencies nationwide. RSVP volunteers serve in courts, schools, museums, libraries, hospices, hospitals, nursing homes, and other service centers. They may be reimbursed for transportation expenses. Current RSVP projects emphasize services to youths, literacy, drug abuse, in-home care, consumer education, crime prevention, and management assistance to private nonprofit and public agencies.

SCORE
1129 20th Street, N.W., Suite 410
Washington, DC 20036 • (202) 653-6279 and (800) 368-5855

SCORE is the acronym for the Service Corps of Retired Executives, a 12,500-member association of volunteers who work out of 592 locations in every state of the nation. SCORE is sponsored by the U.S. Small Business Administration and funded with $2.1 million annually. Members counsel people wanting to go into business or to expand existing businesses, and helps those in financial trouble. Counseling is always free, though a small charge is made for workshops. SCORE was established in 1964 and handles about 620,000 clients annually.

Senior Companion Program • ACTION
806 Connecticut Avenue, N.W., Room 1006
Washington, DC 20525 • (202) 634-9351 and (800) 424-8867

In the Senior Companion Program (SCP)—run by AC-
TION, the federal domestic volunteer agency—low-income
Americans aged sixty and older provide personalized assistance to older adults in need of care and companionship. In
1986, approximately 5,300 Companions helped 18,600
clients achieve their highest level of independent living.
Through 97 SCP projects, volunteers gave more than 5.6
million hours to clients who are homebound and at risk of
being institutionalized. Senior Companions, who work 20
hours per week, receive a stipend of $2.20 per hour, meals,
transportation assistance, and insurance.

Notes

1: *Bringing More Joy and Fulfillment to Your Life*

1. Henri J. Nouwen, *Lifesigns*, Doubleday, 1986, p. 86.

2. *Giving and Volunteering in the United States*, 1988 Edition, Independent Sector, 1828 L Street N.W., Washington D.C. 20036.

3. *The Denver Post*, "Neighborliness at Home on the Range," by Jim Carrier, May 29, 1989.

4. Marsha Sinetar, *Ordinary People as Monks and Mystics*, Paulist Press, Copyright © 1986, pp. 66-67.

5. *San Francisco Chronicle*, "The Good Samaritan Glut," by Liz Lufkin, February 27, 1989. © *San Francisco Chronicle*. Reprinted by permission.

6. From *How Can I Help?* by Ram Dass and Paul Gorman. Copyright © 1985 by Ram Dass and Paul Gorman. Reprinted by permission of Alfred A. Knopf, Inc.

2: *Helping Others When You're Busy*

1. Lyman Randall, *Notes from Midlife*, Freeman Farms Press, Orchard Park, New York, 1986, p. 11.

2. Thornton Wilder, *Our Town: A Play in Three Acts*, Harper & Row, 1985.

3. Marlene Wilson, *Survival Skills for Managers*, Chapter V, Volunteer Management Associates, 320 S. Cedar Brook Road, Boulder, Colorado, 80304, 1981.

4. Reprinted from *The Caring Question* by Donald and

Nancy Tubesing. Copyright © 1983 Augsburg Publishing House. Used by permission of Augsburg Fortress.

5. John Naisbitt, *Megatrends: Ten New Directions Transforming Our Lives*, Warner Books, 1982, pp. 232, 247.

6. From *How Can I Help?* by Ram Dass and Paul Gorman. Copyright © 1985 by Ram Dass and Paul Gorman. Reprinted by permission of Alfred A. Knopf, Inc.

7. Phillip Berman, *The Courage of Conviction*, Ballantine Books, 1985, p. 124.

8. *The Washington Post*, "Taking Time to Give Time," by Neal Karlen, March 3, 1989.

9. "Together—A Company and its Communities," published by General Dynamics Corporation, p. 64.

10. "Together—A Company and its Communities," p. 29.

11. *The Washington Post Magazine*, "Unsung Heroes," by Karlyn Barker, December 24, 1989.

12. Phillip Berman, p. 176.

13. Mother Teresa, *Words to Love by*, Ave Maria Press, 1983, pp. 7, 79.

3: Reaching Out When You're Lonely Or In Transition

1. Lyman Randall, *Notes from Midlife*, Freeman Farms Press, Orchard Park, New York, 1986, pp. 46-47.

2. Dag Hammarskjold, *Markings*, Alfred A. Knopf, 1964, p. 174.

3. Leo Buscaglia, *Living, Loving & Learning*, Slack, Inc., 1982, pp. 200-201.

4. *Newsweek*, "A Salute to Everyday Heroes," July 10, 1989, p. 63.

5. Bill Berkowitz, *Local Heroes*, Lexington Books, 1987, pp. 126-127, 131.

6. *Voluntary Action Leadership*, published by VOLUNTEER: The National Center, 1111 North 19th Street, Suite 500, Arlington, Virginia 22209, "Jacksonville Singles Find Volunteering on the 'Upbeat'," Winter 1986, p. 10.

7. Reprinted from *The Caring Question* by Donald and Nancy Tubesing. Copyright © 1983 Augsburg Publishing House. Used by permission of Augsburg Fortress.

8. Dr. Robert S. Eliot and Dennis L. Breo, *Is It Worth Dying For?*, Bantam Books, 1984.

9. From *Windows* by Jennifer James, Ph.D. Copyright © 1987 Jennifer James. Reprinted by permission of Newmarket Press, 18 E. 48 St., New York, NY 10017.

4: Learning and Growing Through Sharing

1. Abraham Maslow, *Toward a Psychology of Being*, New York: Van Nostrand, Copyright © 1968, p. 201.

2. *U.S. News & World Report*, "Volunteer Jobs with Solid Payoffs," by Terri Thompson and Sharon Golden, April 24, 1989, pp. 76-77.

3. *The Washington Post*, "Taking Time to Give Time," by Neal Karlen, March 3, 1989.

4. Roger von Oech, *A Kick in the Seat of the Pants*, Harper & Row, 1986.

5. *The Forgotten Half: Pathways to Success for America's Youth and Young Families, Youth and America's Future*, The Wil-

liam T. Grant Commission on Work, Family and Citizenship, November 1988. (Full report available for $15 from "Youth and America's Future," Suite 301, 1001 Conneticut Ave., N.W., Washington D.C. 20036-5541.)

6. *MOVS*, "Volunteers Move Minnesota," Vol. 14, No. 2, 1989, Minnesota Office of Volunteer Service.

7. *Voluntary Action Leadership*, published by VOLUNTEER: The National Center, Fall 1988.

8. *The Wall Street Journal*, "Penn Law School Move on Pro Bono Work Courts Public Service in Young Lawyers," by Milo Gezelin, May 22, 1989.

9. *Voluntary Action Leadership*, Summer 1986.

5: Putting Your Beliefs Into Action

1. *The Lutheran Standard*, "You're Asking Me What Poverty Is!," June 11, 1968, p. 5.

2. Henri Nouwen, *With Open Hands*, Ballantine Books, 1985, p. 43.

3. Elizabeth O'Connor, *Eighth Day of Creation*, Word Books, 1971, p. 43.

4. Paul Scherer, *Love is a Spendthrift*, Bantam Books, 1972, p. 52.

5. Mother Teresa, *Words to Love by*, Ave Maria Press, 1983.

6. Phillip Berman, *The Courage of Conviction*, Ballantine Books, 1985, pp. 225-237.

7. Phillip Berman, p. 16.

8. Earl A. Loomis, *The Self in Pilgrimage*, Harper & Row,

1960, pp. 6-7.

9. Richard Foster, *Celebration of Discipline*, Harper & Row, 1978, pp. 117-122.

10. Henri Nouwen, *The Wounded Healer*, Doubleday, 1979.

11. From *Family Faith Stories* by Ann Weems. Copyright © 1985 Ann Weems. Used by permission of Westminster/John Knox Press.

6: Helping a Cause You Care About

1. *Guideposts Magazine*, "What One Person Can Do," by Norman Vincent Peale, April 1973, p. 13. Reprinted with permission from *Guideposts Magazine*. Copyright © 1973 by Guideposts Associates, Inc., Carmel, NY 10512.

2. *Giving and Volunteering in the United States*, 1988 edition, Gallup Survey conducted for Independent Sector, 1928 L Street N.W., Washington D.C. 20036, p. 7.

3. *Newsweek*, "A First Lady Who Cares," by Barbara Kantrowitz and Ann McDaniel, July 10, 1989, pp. 43-44.

4. *Parade*, "Everything Would Be Better If More People Could Read," by Edward Klein, May 21, 1989, pp. 4-6.

5. *Sentinel* (Milwaukee, Wisconsin), "Miracle on 27th St. Provides Hope, Shelter to Needy Families," by Mary Beth Murphy, December 24, 1988.

6. Bill Berkowitz, *Local Heroes*, Lexington Books, 1987, pp. 237-246.

7. *Boulder Daily Camera*, "The Gospel of Living by Daddy Bruce," by Dave Jackson, January 1, 1989.

8. *The Pittsburgh Press*, "Dreams Come True," by Noreen

Subocher.

9. *Parade*, "Men Who Love Babies," by Bill Gale, December 24, 1989.

10. Bill Berkowitz, pp. 149-166.

11. Bill Berkowitz, pp. 272-291.

12. *Newsweek*, "A Salute to Everyday Heroes," July 10, 1989, p. 46.

13. "Together—A Company and its Communities," published by General Dynamics Corporation, pp. 42-43.

7: Sharing Your Lifetime Experience

1. "What Lies Ahead: Looking Toward the '90s," a United Way of America Study, 1987, p. 49.

2. Gail Sheehy, *Passages*, E. P. Dutton, 1974, p. 20.

3. From *Windows* by Jennifer James, Ph.D. Copyright © 1987 Jennifer James. Reprinted by permission of Newmarket Press, 18 E. 48 St., New York, NY 10017.

4. Most of these quotations came from: William Safir and Leonard Safir, *Words of Wisdom*, Simon & Schuster, 1989.

5. *American Health*, "The Immunity of Samaritans: Beyond Self," by Eileen Rockefeller Growald and Allan Luks, March 1988, pp. 51-53.

6. *The Executive Speechwriter Newsletter*, Joe Taylor Ford, Editor, Volume 3, Number 3, p. 4.

7. *Newsweek*, "A Salute to Everyday Heroes," July 10, 1989, p. 59.

8. *Newsweek*, p. 49.

9. *Volunteer Alabama*, "Governor Lauds 'Mother' to Homeless," by Courtenay Miles, Spring/Summer 1989, p. 3.

10. *AARP News Bulletin*, "Helping 'em Get it Right," by Ilene Springer, December 1989, p. 16.

11. *Kenosha News*, "Ethnic Elder Program Aids Minorities," by Jennie Tunkieicz, May, 20, 1989.

8: Giving to Others When You Have Less

1. From *How Can I Help?* by Ram Dass and Paul Gorman. Copyright © 1985 by Ram Dass and Paul Gorman. Reprinted by permission of Alfred A. Knopf, Inc.

2. *Voluntary Action Leadership*, published by VOLUNTEER: The National Center, Winter, 1986.

3. Marge Simonds, *It Occurred to Me*, Volunteer Management Associates, 320 S. Cedar Brook Road, Boulder, CO 80304, 1983.

9: Impacting the Future

1. Ken Dychtwald, Ph.D., *Age Wave: How the Most Important Trend of Our Time Will Change Your Future*, Bantam Books, 1990, pp. 6, 8.

2. *The Washington Post*, "Oprah, Winningly," by Barbara Feinman.

3. *The Executive Speechwriter Newsletter*, Joe Taylor Ford, Editor.

4. Dychtwald, pp. 4-6.

5. Dychtwald, p. 30.

6. Dychtwald, pp. 147, 157-158.

Appendix A: Volunteer Centers

1. *1989 Volunteer Center Associate Member Directory*, Published by VOLUNTEER: The National Center, 1111 N. 19th Street, Suite 500, Arlington, Virginia 22209.

Appendix B: Opportunities for Seniors

1. John F. Raynolds III and Eleanor Raynolds CBE, *Beyond Success*, Master Media Limited, 1988, pp. 131-134.